STOP WALKING YOUR DOG

A GUIDE TO TRAINING YOUR NERVOUS, REACTIVE, OR OVER-EXCITED PUP

NIKI FRENCH

authors
AND CO.

CONTENTS

DEDICATION

*For the incredible force of nature that is Ash, aka Tigger, aka The Noise,
Chris Ashworth. As two people we couldn't be more different or more
complementary. Thank you for leading the way in not settling for anything
less than doing something that fills your heart every single day. And thank
you for embracing games-based training and growing the most incredible
relationship with Bodie.*

For Bodie, our very over-excitable Battersea Rescue dog. One of his many nicknames is Lemon Juice - he's so beautiful it hurts your eyes. He's a massive part of Pup Talk and is always up for working with me when the filming tripod comes out.

For my dog training and life inspirations Tom Mitchell and Lauren Langman. Thank you for showing me how different dog training and running a business can be and creating an amazing community where I know I belong.

For my mum for being, obviously, the best mum in the world and also being a fabulous virtual assistant and proofreader for anything I ask for help with. You are truly special.

For all the dog-lovers past, present and future that work with me, facing their struggles and growing their relationships with their pups. Thank you for trusting me to help you.

INTRODUCTION

"SURELY DOGS KNOW HOW TO GO FOR A WALK!?"

"You get a dog, and you walk them twice a day, that's what you do."

"All dogs love their walks."

"If you're having any trouble with your dog, you need to walk them more to tire them out."

"If your dog is pulling/barking/scared/lunging on a walk (fill in as appropriate), you just need to keep at it. They'll get used to it."

"Surely dogs know how to go for a walk!'

Have you heard suggestions and statements like these? How many do you believe? Maybe this is where you are right now? Whatever you are thinking about walks is absolutely fine! There is no judgement here.

When you're having any kind of struggle with your dog, it can really affect how you feel. Are they causing you to feel stressed throughout the day? Are you worried about what they might do at any moment? Do you feel guilty about what you can't do with friends and family because you can't bring your dog with you? Do you feel embarrassed out in public that you have a 'naughty' dog? Have you fallen out with the neighbours over your dog? Do you feel bad for your dog, that you can't let them off the lead wherever you like?

Of course, you love your dog, and you want to do your best for them. But it can feel overwhelming and confusing.

I can show you really practical and easy ways to train your dog. To help them (and you!) live calmer and happier lives.

PART 1

1

WHAT EVEN IS A WALK?

What do your walks look like at the moment?

So, let's be honest now. What do your walks look like recently? Perhaps one of these sounds familiar? Perhaps quite a few of them?

1. You've got a new puppy and now they're vaccinated you want to take them for a walk to help tire them out. They are going crazy at home. Running around, jumping up and nipping, chewing everything. But they just keep sitting down when you try to take them for a walk. Or they're running around in circles, chasing leaves all over the place, picking up sticks or trying to eat stones and rubbish!

2. You might have a dog like mine who wants to excitedly greet everyone and every dog that comes into range. They're likely to be trying to drag you over to them, perhaps pogoing up and down on the lead.

3. Are cats or squirrels making your walks an unpredictable and stressful experience? You are now both well practised at keeping a look out for them (but for quite different reasons).

4. Hands up who has been pulled over on their face (or butt!) by their dog? Even smaller dogs can have you over if you're caught off guard. Perhaps you've even suffered a bone or had some skin taken off while trying to hold onto your dog when something triggered them to try and run when you weren't expecting it.

5. Walks might feel like something you need to 'steel' yourself for. Your dog is scared of other dogs, or strangers, or noises and this means they can react badly and be barking and lunging and nearly pulling you over. You know they're scared but you feel embarrassed that people are judging you for having what can look like 'an aggressive dog', or a 'dog you can't control.'

6. Do you get worried when someone else's off-lead dog rushes up to you and your dog? Perhaps there's the old "don't worry he's friendly" shout from the owner that doesn't seem too bothered that they don't have control of their dog. Perhaps you've even been unfortunate and have experienced another dog attacking yours.

7. Walks might feel like a game of Russian roulette. You spin the 'barrel' and don't know what you're going to get. Some walks are completely fine, others can go pear-shaped in seconds when a dog they're worried about suddenly appears around a corner.

8. Perhaps your dog gets so worried by things outside your home, that they can shut down completely. They're not able to walk on any further, no matter how much hot dog or chicken you try to tempt them with.

9. You might have a dog that is getting older now and not able to go as far. Walks for them are a bit of a stiff waddle and just a slow sniff up and down your road.

10. Are your walks just unpleasant because your pup wants to bark at any dog that they see? Or a person wearing a high visibility jacket or sunglasses, or a rustling bin bag, or someone on a skateboard, scooter or bike? What's on your list? It can be due to excitement or worry, but the effect on you is probably the same.

11. You might have a dog that needs to be on crate rest or restricted

walks following surgery or illness and you want a plan to help everyone get through it with the least amount of stress.

What have you tried so far?

You might have tried puppy classes. You might have found that your puppy could walk on a lead nicely in class and then seem to forget it all when you get back home and head to the park.

Or puppy class might have been rather over-exciting, or a bit scary, and they struggled to learn anything. Perhaps they were barking at the other dogs. You were left feeling like you had the naughty puppy of the group, or you couldn't quite get it right.

If your dog is reactive to other dogs, you might have tried to go on walks to the quietest places you can or go really early in the morning or late at night. The hope is that you don't see any or many other dogs, or that they are far enough away not to cause you any problems. You can't control everything in the environment, so this strategy isn't always successful.

Or you might have just got used to your dog pulling your arm out of its socket. You've tried various combinations of 'no-pull' harnesses, head collars, or other tools, but nothing seems to work like the description on the box. You tried stopping every time they'd pull, but they just keep going back to pulling and you give up and let them pull you because you never get anywhere otherwise.

You might have received some well-meaning but conflicting tips and advice from people you meet. You might have people around you, even in your family/household that aren't supportive of how you want to train your dog.

This just isn't fun

For whatever reason, it might be that you don't look forward to your walks. They are not fun a lot of the time. They can be stressful; they are certainly not relaxing. They are not what you imagined when you thought about having a dog in your life.

If any of this resonates with you, read on!

It doesn't need to feel like this.

I want to replace the old fashioned idea of:

"If you have a dog you take them for a walk once or twice a day."

Yes, all dogs need physical exercise and mental stimulation. But this doesn't have to look like a walk in the traditional sense.

You can replace that idea with:

"I play with my dog, several times a day."

That may or may not include leaving your home and going out for the traditional 'walk.'

Does that sound crazy to you right now? Trust me and go with it!

What even is a walk?

What do your walks look like with your pup? By the way, I use the terms pup to cover a dog or puppy of any age.

You might clip a lead on them and go for a walk around the roads near where you live. Perhaps you're dashing to drop your kids off at school or give the dog some exercise before you start work. Or you might jump in your car and drive out to a park or some woods.

Whatever your 'walk' looks like, it is actually just a loop or a circuit. You open your door, leave your home, go somewhere, and come back. This might sound obvious, but if you're struggling with any aspect of walking your dog, we're going to break down what a walk really is and create something that works for you and your pup.

Yes, a walk can be a great part of growing your relationship and bond with your dog. Yes, it can be great exercise for you and your dog.

It might come as a surprise, but not all dogs have the skills they need to go for a traditional walk. This book talks about the kind of dogs that might be happier not going for a walk and what you can do with them instead. All while you're building up the skills they need to be able to go for a walk, and importantly, enjoy it. A walk shouldn't be something that causes you stress.

Have you wondered if your dog is right for you?

I want you to believe that you are the very best person for your dog (or dogs). No matter what has happened up until now. You have the knowledge you need right here AND the desire to make life different from how it is right now. If you've ever had doubts about whether your dog is for you, or if you are the right person for them - the fact that you're reading this book shows you are THE BEST PERSON FOR THEM.

Having a dog in our lives isn't always easy. People don't tell you that. But dogs are animals, they are sentient beings but they don't speak English (or any other spoken language). Until we teach them the relevance of the noises (words) that we make. And we don't speak dog (at least not until we really study what they are trying to tell us).

You have the support you need. I will support you, with this book and any other ways I can.

So please be kind to yourself if you're reading this because you've been having a hard time - with walks with your dog, or any other aspect of having dogs in your life.

If you've been struggling with any of your dog's behaviour, you might have tried taking them out more to get them tired, or to get them used to whatever it is in the outside world that they struggle with.

If you know anyone else that is struggling with their pup, please tell them about this book. I want as many people as possible to realise they don't have to keep going with challenging walks.

There is another way!

Absolute Dogs? Absolutely me!

What makes me qualified to write this book? Dog training is a whole new career for me that only started in 2018. I spent the previous 30 years working in sales and marketing; for 20 years of that, I was working on residential property.

However, I've been utterly animal-mad, especially dogs, my whole life. I was the feral kid with dirty bare feet, trying to get close to every animal I could. I tried to tame anything from squirrels to New Forest ponies. But, as an adult, regularly working 50-70 hours a week, plus long-haul travel, my life wasn't compatible with having dogs of my own. Before 2019, I didn't have any formal training with dogs, but I always felt instantly that I knew how to 'be' with them.

I was in a bicycle accident in 2014 that started a chain of events that lead to the best decision I have ever made - to leave my old career behind and retrain as a dog trainer and set up my own business.

I did some local work experience and found Absolute Dogs. If you don't know them, Absolute Dogs are the amazing energy that is founders Lauren Langman and Tom Mitchell. Lauren Langman is an incredible dog trainer and world-class agility competitor, winning at Crufts, Olympia and representing Team GB at World Championships. Tom Mitchell BSc BVSc MRCVS is also an incredible dog trainer, veterinarian, and behaviourist, taking on some of the most difficult behaviour cases from all over the world.

Every day, they, and everyone that I've met that is part of the Absolute Dogs family, are a massive inspiration to me. This book is part of the ripple effect I want to have on as many people, and their dogs, as possible. Nearly all the game names, and training frameworks I talk about in this book are directly from Absolute Dogs. Training with them, working alongside so many other Absolute Dogs Pro Dog Trainers, has been amazing. I am so grateful I found them early in my new career.

Sometimes I wish I had changed paths sooner in my life, but then I catch myself and realise that I also needed all the skills that the previous 30 years had given me. This job is not just about being good with dogs - you need to understand and be great with people too. You need to be able to give someone belief and tools so that they can be a great dog trainer for their own dog(s).

I'm still working (slowly) through the Advanced Level 4 Canine Behaviour Diploma. What can I say – setting up a new business, running it single-handed, completely retraining in a new field, launching a podcast, writing a dog, and studying in several different areas means some things don't happen that quickly. I really love that I am relatively fresh to the world of dog training. A lot of what we know about dogs, and how their brains work, has changed in recent years. I'm glad I was pretty much a blank piece of paper only three years ago. It's allowed me to be completely open-minded to new ways of thinking and the latest research.

I urge you to be open-minded too.

I think it also helps me to understand where a lot of my clients are when it comes to their dogs. They're not experts. They just love their dogs and want the best for them. Just like me.

You have got this!

I want you to know that wherever you are right now, you can change how things are with your dog if you need to.

You can find out what you need to know.

You can learn the skills you need.

You can get the help you want.

You are in the right place, right now.

You are THE best person for your dog. Believe in yourself and everything you are capable of.

Instructions on how to use this book

How do you like to read or use a book? I think books are there to be used and the ones I love the most are the ones that look tatty. (Except for a handful of beautiful 'coffee table books' that I have and cherish carefully).

Most books I don't plan to pass on once I've read them. I want to be able to flick back through them and be reminded of any gems that they gave me. Feel free to scribble on this one, highlight bits, bend the corners over (I know that does stress some people out – sorry if that's you!).

I'll be honest, my powers of concentration are not great. Ever since getting knocked off my bicycle in 2014, I struggle to focus for long periods. I find short, clear sections much easier to digest, so that's how I wanted to write this book for you. Plus it means you can flick straight to something that you need without scanning long sections to get to what you want.

If you're like me, you also don't always get to the end of every book. If that is you, I understand! But, if you don't get to the end, do make sure you jump forward to Chapter 15 to read a compilation of my favourite training nuggets so far. These are relevant to EVERY dog guardian.

Please grab any bit of information that speaks to you and help yourself to remember it, in a way that works for you. I want to change what your life looks like with your dog, and habits are ingrained little things that take some effort to change (66 days by all accounts)! You can easily find yourself slipping back to what you've always done or wobble when people challenge what you're doing.

Hold firm and do things differently! Nothing will change unless something changes. I truly hope you enjoy reading this book.

2

WHY WOULDN'T YOU WALK YOUR DOG?

There are lots of reasons <u>not</u> to take our dogs out for a 'walk' as we know it. This Chapter is a quick look at why you could be reading this book and why your current walks might not be helping your dog. The Chapters in Part Two go into more detail on each reason.

Puppies

Puppies simply aren't <u>born</u> with all the skills they need to go for a walk. We need to <u>give</u> them these skills for the outside world. We can teach them what we want them to do on a walk. We need to help them not do things that we don't want them to do (like running in circles, chewing stones and tying us up in knots with the lead).

All of this can happen BEFORE starting walks. This can start from the first week when you've brought your new puppy home. Don't wait, let's get stuck in! See Chapter 7 for more details.

Scared and reactive dogs

Some dogs just really struggle to cope with the environment around them. If your dog is barking and lunging on the lead when they are outside, you probably know that this comes from a place of worry or fear. Whatever the reason for their 'reactivity' the solution is not to expose them to more of what causes them stress and anxiety. By doing this we are constantly putting them in a stressful situation where they are unable to learn what they need. The seemingly 'aggressive' display is their way of trying to make something go away and to change how they feel and from their perspective, this strategy works for them because the cause of their worry has probably moved away, or you and your dog have moved on quickly.

See Chapter 8 for more and let's change the experience for your dog (and you!).

Dogs that are over-excited (jump up and down / pull like a train / bite the lead)

Some dogs are just very excitable and love life, love people, love dogs - anything can be exciting for them.

As much as an excitable dog can look bouncy and happy, it does mean they can be hard work. Jumping up at people, rushing over to other dogs, chewing through the lead, pulling on the lead, or even dragging you over on your face. I know quite a few people that this has happened to, including my partner, Ash, with our dog Bodie!

Excited dogs find it difficult to make good decisions because they're too excited and because they're too excited, they struggle to learn. This makes for a very excitable loop that doesn't seem to get any better.

There is another way – see Chapter 9 for more.

Bitches that are in season

If you've got a bitch in season, for obvious reasons, you might not want to risk off-lead walks. But even on-lead walks can have their challenges.

The drive to mate is a strong instinct and entire males can smell bitches in season from surprising distances. She will also be much more interested in male dogs. Even the most well-trained dogs can struggle when it comes to basic sex drive.

She can also attract the interest of other females. So your dog may feel more anxious with the additional attention she may get.

During their season there are also hormonal changes, which can affect their behaviour. They can be more alert or reactive, or value resources more highly. This means an increased risk of an incident over food or toys with other dogs around.

See Chapter 10 for more specific help.

Physical restrictions for our dogs or us

There are various physical reasons that our dogs might not be capable of going for a walk. These include when recovering from surgery or an injury, or it could be deteriorating health and mobility, possibly associated with old age.

There could also be periods when we have less mobility through injury or illness. My own recent broken foot made me look at training games to adapt to play seated at home, and I couldn't write this book in 2021 without talking about movement restrictions placed on many of us around the world, due to the global pandemic.

See Chapter 11 for ways to get flexible with the exercise and brain games.

3

WHY DOES MY DOG DO THAT?

What we know about dogs and how their brains work, has changed a lot in recent years, but if you take a little time to understand what makes your dog do what he or she does, it can really help your relationship with them. It will also help them to live a calmer and happier life.

Your dog's brain

Let's start with your dog's brain. In the words of Tom Mitchell, Absolute Dogs:

> "Every dog has a brain!"

It's useful to think of their brain as being made up of lots of different building blocks. Each one of these blocks represents part of their personality. Each one of these blocks is a concept.

A concept is simply a general principle we want our dogs to understand. And be able to understand in lots of different situations. These concepts are what influence your dog to do what they do. It's what makes up their personality; who they are. With all the things we love about them and the things we wished they didn't do.

Every dog is different. They will have some parts of their personality (concepts) that are strengths and some that are weaknesses.

They all have strengths even if you might see something as a weakness, i.e. a dog that might not have great recall, probably has the strength of **independence**! But don't worry too much about their weaknesses, we can change this!

Let's look at a few examples of the concepts and what they might look like.

You may have a very **confident** dog; confident with strangers, new dogs, new places. Fantastic! This is a great strength to have. But it may mean that they are a bit too eager to run over and introduce themselves to people in the park.

You may have a dog that isn't confident, at least some of the time and this can look like a dog that barks at other dogs or people. They are hoping for the other dog or person to move away or leave them alone.

Calmness is one of my favourite concepts - a calm dog is a wonderful thing. Before you got your dog what did you imagine life would be like? Snuggles on the sofa watching Netflix? Or having them curl up under the table in a dog-friendly pub while you sip an espresso martini? That's not just me, is it? If you've already got a calm dog, that's amazing. But if you're reading this book, I'm guessing your dog isn't calm all of the time.

Puppies are very unlikely to be calm (unless they're sleeping). There are a few exceptions, but not many.

The concept of **disengagement** is something a lot of dogs struggle with. Disengagement is the ability to see enough value in coming away from something. It might be something they find exciting or scary. If your dog is walking along with its nose permanently on the ground, he or she can't disengage from all the amazing smells. If your dog can't stop playing with other dogs in the park, they can't **disengage** from the dogs and **engage** with you.

Novelty is the ability to be confident with things that are new or ambiguous. What is a great reaction from our dogs? No significant reaction at all. It's not worrying or exciting to them even though they haven't seen it before or they're not sure what it is.

Our dogs are naturally curious (it comes from a survival instinct) and we don't want to suppress their reactions. But we want to give them the tools so that they don't feel the need to over-react.

Optimism is a concept that can really help our dogs not to be worried by new situations. They can learn that just because something is unfamiliar doesn't mean it's bad. Pessimism was a useful survival concept for early dogs when there were animals that could eat them. It's not so relevant now! But many of our dogs are still natural pessimists that get worried.

Proximity is the concept of our dogs seeing and understanding the value of hanging out with us, right next to us. If a dog loves proximity, they are not pulling on the lead. If a dog loves proximity, then recall becomes a doddle. Of course, they come back to you, no matter what, that's where they love to be!

These are just a few of the concepts to get you started. We'll cover more once we get in to 'How to' part of the book.

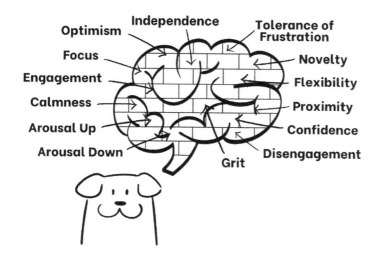

The beauty of concept training is we can grow the weak concepts and turn them into strengths. We can actually reshape our dogs' brains. What!?!

Yes, we can. Then they can make better decisions themselves without us needing to tell them what to do. How amazing is that!

This is a key difference between concept training and more traditional training. If you have a dog that jumps up at the kitchen counter/worktop to see if there is some food up there, you can:

Scenario A. Teach them an 'Off' or 'Down' cue to stop them each time they do it. But what happens when you're not there? I've seen those TikTok videos of dogs having a party on the kitchen counter!

Or...

Scenario B. Grow their personality (the right concepts) so that they choose not to jump up at the kitchen worktop, whether you are there or not. (**Calmness** and **disengagement** would be a good place to start with this example).

So scenario A is teaching our dogs tricks or behaviours that they do on cue.

Scenario B goes way deeper than that. Once we identify the weak concepts that your dog needs help with, we can target them and turn them into strengths.

What we can control (and what we can't)

Life is made up of events. Some we can control, but many that we can't.

What is important to our dogs and their behaviour is, if an event happens – are they aware of it? If they're not aware of something, it's not relevant to them.

If they are aware of something (any event, say seeing another dog), the brain processes it and then their brain decides on an outcome. How your dog reacts to the event, very much depends on those concepts (the strengths and weaknesses).

That outcome could be:

1. *See a dog they are worried about* > bark and lunge on the lead.

Or

2. *See a dog they're excited to see* > jump up and pull on the lead to try and drag you over to see them.

Or

3. *See a dog, not be too bothered* and just carry on walking calmly along with you.

If the picture with your dog is currently looking more like number 1 or 2, know that you can reshape their brain with the right training games to get to number 3.

Yes, we can control some things. We can choose to walk in quiet places, early in the morning or late at night to try and limit the likelihood of us meeting other dogs or too many people. But you can't control everything. Sometimes you might have someone appear round the corner with a dog or have someone on a bike quietly cycle up behind you before you spotted it.

Life happens. And while you can't control everything in the environment around your dog, you can reshape their brain. And if you reshape their brain, they can make different decisions. If they make a different decision, you can change the outcome from the events that happen.

Wow! That stills blows my mind how much dog training has moved on. But there is still not enough people in mainstream media talking about this. If this is new to you, know that it can change so much for you and your dog.

So no matter what your dog is like, whatever their personality is right now, you can change what the picture looks like. I hope this makes you feel excited!

A word on management

In addition to helping your dog learn new skills, the best way to help them learn is to manage behaviours that you don't like or don't want. This means not letting them practise behaviours. This could be pulling on the lead, barking, jumping up, running over to other dogs or people, humping etc.

Every single time you let your dog pull on the lead, they get used to doing it.

Every time you leave them in the garden, and they bark at birds in the tree, or your neighbour's dog, they get better at it.

Every time you giggle at your puppy humping their bed or a soft toy, they are practising it.

Some of these behaviours feel good! And they're doing them because they are trying to change the way they feel. Or to cope with how they feel.

With any behaviour, imagine what it will be like in a year or two if they are still doing it? Or doing it even more. Does that match your vision for the future? If not, do something about it now.

I know this can take quite a lot of vigilance and effort but the more you put the time in now, the quicker you will be able to step back from dealing with it because they have learned other things to do instead. Other ways of coping with an emotion, or not feeling the need to do it to release excitement or stress.

Here are some examples of how to manage common struggles:

Your puppy is humping their bed	You could remove the bed and make them a bed out of a veg box with a folded up towel in it. No, they really won't mind, and you can save the lovely plush bed that you bought until they don't want to hump it or chew it!
Your puppy is chewing things they shouldn't	Puppy proof any area they have access to. They are exploring the world with their mouth or easing teething pains. Make sure they don't have access to anything you don't want to be chewed. Or supervise them when they have more access. Or pop them in a crate or 'puppy proofed' room (as long as your puppy can relax in this environment). A kitchen, bathroom or utility room can be easier to make safe for them.
Your puppy is struggling with toilet training and pees on the rug or your bed	Don't let them have free access to areas where they are making mistakes. It's your responsibility to help them only go where you want them to. Either, watch them like a hawk if they have access to a larger area or, have them in a crate or pen when you can't watch them. Take them to the toileting area very regularly and celebrate every successful visit!
Your dog is digging in the garden	Don't leave them unattended in the garden or make the area that they dig inaccessible. You can get creative with garden furniture, tables on their sides and sturdy plant pots depending on the size of your dog and your garden. Sandpits are also a great way to channel this very natural dog behaviour; teach them where they can dig.
Your dog isn't reliable off the lead	Don't let them off the lead yet! Use a longline to give them some freedom while still giving you control of where and how far they go.
Your dog barks at birds/wildlife/cats etc. in the garden	Don't leave them unattended in the garden. Play DMT (Distraction Mark Treat) when you are supervising them (see Chapter 12 for details).
Your dog is reactive and scared of other dogs or people	Stop taking your dog out where there is any potential to see dogs (or people) that could worry them. Grow the skills they need at home first.
Your dog gets excited and boisterous with other dogs	Don't let them off the lead around other dogs or, if their recall is 100%, you could let them play for a very short time (with the other person's permission of course), and then pop them back on the lead after a short period before it gets too exciting. But do be aware some dogs can find interactions with other dogs more of a challenge when they are on the lead. You have a choice about which dogs (if any) they get to interact with.
Your dog jumps at visitors in your home	Put them in another room, on a lead or in their crate before your visitors arrive. You can give them a lick mat or a long-lasting chew or a calming game. If they are calm enough, you might want to allow some controlled greetings. But don't feel you have to.

Yes, you do have to weigh up the effort it takes to manage your individual situations but think of the time you spend as an investment in a much easier life further down the line. You will be so grateful you did! I promise.

Did you know your dog has a bucket?

Did you know your dog has a **bucket**? Well, a metaphorical one anyway. It's a useful way to think about our dogs' arousal levels, and by arousal, I'm talking about the hormone **cortisol**. Dogs need cortisol in their systems to be alive, but like us, too much isn't a good thing.

How much cortisol our dogs can handle (the size of their bucket) in a day varies significantly. Some dogs have a really big bucket and very little bothers them. These are chilled out gems! Other dogs can really struggle even with small amounts of stress and excitement in their day; they have a very small bucket. The size of their bucket is completely unrelated to the physical size of the dog. A Chihuahua can have a massive bucket, and a Bernese Mountain Dog can have a very small bucket.

This arousal bucket also has a hole in the bottom so that the cortisol is draining away over time. Again this might be a big or a small hole - the bigger the hole the easier and quicker the cortisol drains away.

On a daily basis, it is helpful to think about how full your dog's bucket is. For example, if they had a particularly exciting or worrying event in the morning, we can use this information to adapt what we do later that day, or the next day.

What is filling up our dogs' buckets each day? There are lots of both positive and negative things.

Positive bucket fillers

- Excitement – in my household this is an Amazon delivery or a visitor! (Well, it is 2021 and we didn't really have any visitors for 18 months in the pandemic lockdown.)
- Fast play – perhaps chasing games or tug.
- Fast-moving games – some games are great for boosting recall, but they can be very exciting.
- Fun dog sports like hoopers, agility and flyball.
- Constantly being on the go – do they live in a busy household, or do they struggle to switch off and rest?
- Predictable routine – although routine isn't specifically negative, it can still pay into the bucket. A routine means your dog learns to anticipate what's coming up (perhaps set mealtimes or a walk). Their growing excitement for the event that they are predicting is coming up, raising their stress levels.

Negative bucket fillers

- Frustration – not being able to get to you because you need to get some work done at home.
- Worrying events – a trip to the vets.
- Fear – having a strange dog rush up to them when you're on a walk.
- Anxiety – being left home alone and they struggle with separation issues.
- Pain – any kind of short or long term pain is a big bucket filler. We might not even be aware of it.
- Itchiness – if your dog scratches more than once or twice a day, this isn't normal, and they could be feeling itchy. Itching can also be a behavioural response when your dog is feeling stressed.
- Gastrointestinal (GI) upset – sickness and diarrhoea unsurprisingly are on the list.

So each day lots of small events can be adding a cupful into your dog's arousal bucket. Or one or two big things can happen. What's significant is what happens when the bucket is full to overflowing. This is when a dog finds it virtually impossible to make a good decision. Have you ever experienced something with your dog when everything seemed fine in the morning? Their recall was good, or they were walking nicely on the lead and then later that day (or even later on in the same walk) they are like a different dog! They couldn't or wouldn't listen. People say to me: "It's like they go completely deaf on me!"

This is an overflowing bucket and by being aware of it we can make good decisions for our dogs. Perhaps we don't let them off the lead in the afternoon, instead, we go for a lovely sniffy walk or perhaps we don't go for a walk at all and play some scent games at home.

At the same time as helping to avoid an overflowing arousal bucket, we can be playing the right training games to help grow a bigger bucket with a nice big hole in the bottom!

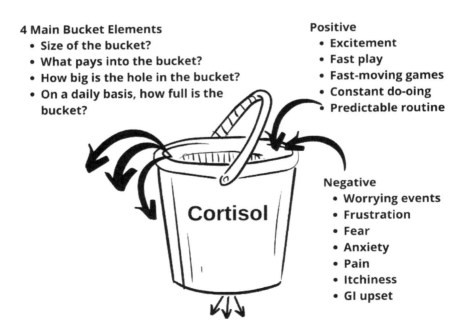

4 Main Bucket Elements
- Size of the bucket?
- What pays into the bucket?
- How big is the hole in the bucket?
- On a daily basis, how full is the bucket?

Positive
- Excitement
- Fast play
- Fast-moving games
- Constant do-oing
- Predictable routine

Cortisol

Negative
- Worrying events
- Frustration
- Fear
- Anxiety
- Pain
- Itchiness
- GI upset

BUILD THE SKILLS AT HOME

If you're reading this book, you are probably having some 'challenges' with your dog when they are out on a walk or in the park. If this is the case, you need to build up the skills at home. Before you even step out of the front door.

We want to train our dogs for the event, not be trying to train them when the event is happening. We want to give them the skills they need before they need them.

You wouldn't train for a marathon by running a marathon. You would probably make a plan and get some advice from people with experience. At the very least you would prepare yourself by building up bit by bit the amount of running you did and you'd probably do other exercises, stretching and massage to prepare your body. So set yourself up with the best possible chance of finishing a marathon without doing yourself an injury. (And it would probably still be quite hard).

Anyone that knows me, knows I'll never run a marathon (dodgy knees and feet for starters!). Not everyone is made to run marathons. Likewise, not all dogs are cut out to go on walks. Some dogs might never enjoy them and that's OK.

Dog training advice used to be (and still is, in some cases) – expose your dog to something they need to work on (whether scared, anxious, over-excited etc.). If it's something that they react badly to, you'd probably be told to go to a distance that they can just about cope with it and then get closer and closer to the 'stimulus' (the thing they need to work on).

Or it could be, take your puppy to puppy classes and try to teach them there. Imagine a field or church hall with 6 to 8 puppies in it. Some puppies are very over-excited, some are nervous. Some people are feeling a bit stressed and anxious because they seem to have the 'naughty puppy' or the one that can't concentrate and learn anything.

Both of these examples are pretty much like training for a marathon by jumping straight in and running one. That wouldn't work; the likelihood of you finishing wouldn't be high and even if you managed to finish, it would probably be a bit painful and you wouldn't want to do it again!

Dogs find it harder to learn positive things when they are over-excited, stressed, or anxious. When a dog's body is dealing with raised levels of cortisol, the non-essential functions are down-regulated. This includes digestion - no wonder they're not interested in food all of a sudden. It even affects their immune system (in case you needed any incentive to keep reading about your dog's bucket).

Unhelpfully, stress makes it easier to learn from unpleasant experiences. So, if they are scared of a dog or person passing their window and they bark, and the object of their worry goes away, they quickly learn that barking works to get rid of something that scares them! They don't know that the dog or person was just walking past anyway. By working on concept training, you can build the skills your dog needs, before you even start to expose them to the scary or overly exciting thing.

If your dog is scared of noises in the outside world (say lorries and trucks), there are games you can play at home. They are probably more relaxed in familiar surroundings, and they can learn the skills they need (**confidence** around games with other noises).

Have you got a dog that is constantly pulling you when you're out on a walk? If so, we can build up their love of being right by your side (**proximity**).

There are normally several concepts that will help to work together. We'll go into more specific struggles, and the corresponding concepts to work on, in later Chapters.

All you need to know right now is that concept training gets amazing results. You may be surprised just how effective it can be to play a game at home that doesn't seem close enough to the thing they are struggling with. But it works! For thousands of dogs. For every type of dog.

Have you got a dog that's completely over-excited and wants to jump up and greet everyone and everything? **Calmness** is what they need more of.

Calmness is one of the most interesting concepts. Traditional dog training doesn't talk much about it, if at all. Yet growing **calmness** can be fundamental in helping so many of the struggles our dogs have (and therefore our struggles!).

Picture what a calm dog looks like. I'll describe my sister's wonderful Westie, Fergus. He was born calm. He is the most laid-back cool dog you can imagine. He would trot around at his own pace. Not too bothered by anyone or anything. Happy to settle at your feet and just get an ear scruffle.

Calm dogs don't jump up at people or the kitchen counter. Calm dogs don't bark at passers-by or birds in the garden or drag you along the street from lamppost to lamppost.

Most puppies don't know how to be calm. They're not born with the natural skill (concept) of **calmness**. A lot of the challenging puppy behaviours come from being over-excited. The jumping up, biting, mouthing and it generally gets worse when they're over-tired and over-exercised.

Think about the struggles you might be having with your dog. What does the opposite look like? Often the opposite is **calmness**. In an ideal world, we don't want to put our dogs into situations and environments where they feel the need to be over-excited or scared.

Calmness can be a 'bottleneck' – the concept that makes the other struggles reduce, or even disappear. Because the concept is so powerful, and so many dogs can benefit from learning to be calm more of the time, it has its own Chapter.

Fergus, the calmest dog I've ever met. I think many dogs could benefit from being a bit more Fergus.

5

GOOD FOUNDATIONS - THE CALMNESS WHEEL

If you only take one thing away from this book, let it be that **calmness** is sooooooo important! With pretty much every struggle, working on your dog's ability to be calm will help. Unless you've got a 'Fergus'. And even then, you'll find some useful information in this Chapter so no skipping past this one.

The calmness wheel is a training framework to give you a whole variety of tools to help your puppy or dog be calmer, more of the time, and in lots of different situations.

The calmness wheel is divided into three parts.

1. Passive calming – it's passive because you are not doing anything, while it is calming for your dog.
2. The calmness protocol – things you can do to help grow calmness.
3. Rest – you may be surprised but not all dogs know how to rest.

1. Passive calming

Passive calming means it's passive for you – because, once you've set it up, you don't need to be involved and it's calming for your dog. I'm going to go through a wide variety of passive calming activities here because it's so useful to build these activities into your dog's day for EVERY kind of dog. Every age. Every breed. Every behaviour struggle they might have.

These are all activities that can occupy your dog for some time with something tasty. Or that involves using their nose. A couple of the brilliant benefits of some passive calming activities is the dog is either licking, chewing, or sniffing. Both of these have a naturally calming effect on the dog. They are also using combinations of their sense of smell, eyesight, and a lot of brain power.

These activities are great for getting a pup of any age ready to settle down. It might be before they need to have a nap or go to bed for the night. Or before you go out. Or to create a lovely calm association with a crate, bed, quiet room, even the car.

Passive calming activities can also be used to effectively redirect a dog that is doing something that you don't want them to. Just telling our dogs not to do something doesn't tell them what we want them to do instead. They might want to jump up at us and mouth our arms. If we say 'No!' in a stern voice, they could stop briefly, but then start again. Or go and find something else to do - that we also don't want. Like chewing the chair leg or digging a hole.

They need to do something at that moment, and they don't yet know a good choice to make.

As well as helping to calm excitement, passive calming activities can also really help dogs when they are feeling anxious. As long as they are not 'over-threshold' (an instantly full bucket). There comes a point at which a dog is too worried or anxious to eat, no matter how tasty something is.

If we can use passive calming activities when our dogs are slightly worried or anxious, we can grow their **calmness** and **confidence** with what they can cope with.

These activities are also really useful for situations where your pup struggles. Here are just a few situations that I would use passive calming activities for:

- They get really over-excited when you have friends over.
- A delivery arrival is due and knocking at the door sets your dog off barking or jumping at the window.
- Recycling/bin day.
- You've got work going on in your home or garden or next door.
- You'd like to be able to eat breakfast or dinner without interruptions.
- You'd like to be able to go out and meet a friend for a drink and have your dog curl up quietly under the table.

There are so many uses for passive calming activities! Make a list of times when your dog struggles to be calm. What do you notice? Are there any patterns about times of day or activities that are harder for them to deal with?

If we redirect them onto one of the calming activities coming up, we are showing them what we want them to do instead. Passive calming activities help bring down their excitement (and/or anxiety levels). It is going to be helping to empty their bucket.

By doing these activities daily we are getting our dogs used to being calm more of the time - we're growing the size of their bucket. This means they can cope with more of what modern life throws at them without their bucket overflowing. They get into the habit of being calm. Amazingly, this can happen with something that is pretty low maintenance when it comes to your time.

This is not training that takes up hours of your day. You will need to supervise them with anything new to start with but for most of these activities, you can just leave them to it. Meaning you are free to get on with whatever you need to do.

Feel free to get a pen or highlighter out and scribble all over these pages. What ideas sound easy for you to do? Perhaps you've tried some of them, but you've spotted some new ideas you want to try.

If you've got any favourites that aren't on this list, I'd love to hear them. Drop me an email at info@puptalk.co.uk

Scatter feeding

Scatter feeding has to be one of the easiest and most effective passive calming activities. I use it daily with Bodie.

You simply take some of their daily food allowance and scatter it on the floor. That's it! Then encourage them to eat it (if you need to).

You can scatter inside – anywhere you're happy to do a sweep up of a few crumbs afterwards. You can use a patio, balcony, a garden, on a quiet path on your walk, in a park. Anywhere...

(If you feed exclusively raw or wet food, have a look at Chapter 6 for more ideas that can work for you.)

Start by putting a few pieces down in a small area and encourage your dog to get them. You can get involved with a 'find it' cue if you want to. Even for puppies, scatter feeding is fine, just make it really easy to start, with the food close together.

After the first few times, and once you know that your dog is happily sniffing about to find the food, you can just leave them to it. You can get on with getting your breakfast or whatever else you need to do. It will depend on how much food you use, and how quick your dog is. Some dogs will be done in a minute, others will be going back over the area, again and again, to make sure they haven't missed a bit.

I like to mix up the food I give Bodie. Now I really like chocolate, but if you gave it to me every meal of every day, I probably wouldn't enjoy it as much. If you're feeding your dog the same food all the time, they can get bored of it. Or at least not be as motivated by it.

By having different smells and flavours scattered over an area, it is more likely to get the dog working their way around all the different pieces of food to see which ones they want to eat first.

Some dogs (yes you Labradors – I see you) will just hoover it all up as quickly as possible. But it's still going to take longer than a normal bowl or slow feeder.

So, unless you've got a very foodie dog, I would suggest you try using mostly their daily 'normal' food with a few tastier bits in there as well.

Once Bodie has searched out the best bits, he'll happily crunch on his kibble. If I just scattered the kibble down, he wouldn't always be that interested in it.

What we are doing is **creating an experience** for our dogs. Dogs didn't evolve with a nice shiny bowl of food in the corner of our kitchens tens of thousands of years ago. They had to search for food using all of their senses. By the time they have 'found' each piece of food, it tastes better because they had to work for it! This has a name if you're interested – contra freeloading. There is more on this in Chapter 6.

During this time, they are using their senses and their brain. It is much more mentally tiring for them to eat this way and mentally tired is a GREAT thing! zzzZZ

Scatter feeding has so many benefits:

- For dogs that eat their food quickly, it sloooows them right down.
- You don't need to buy a special slow feeder bowl. For very foodie dogs, you can spread the food over quite a wide area.

- For dogs that are not that into their food, it can help them become more 'foodie'.
- For dogs that struggle to be away from you, this gives them a lovely calm activity to do while you have a little space between you. You're working on the concept of **independence** right there, without even trying.
- For dogs that struggle with distractions, it can give them a calming activity to focus on that helps build up their ability to cope with the distraction. For example, Bodie would woof at the pigeons flapping around in the trees around our garden. With a tasty scatter feed he can be aware of the pigeons but is a bit too busy eating to be bothered by them.

People worry that you are going to create a dog that is encouraged to start scavenging for food. Don't worry. You are giving them a focused outlet to eat in a natural way. You can put a cue on this activity like 'find it' if you want to. Dogs want to do natural dog behaviours; this is showing them a way to do it that you approve of.

You can use it for a number of different struggles.

If your dog gets over-excited in the middle of a walk, perhaps they're pulling on the lead or jumping around. You can stop and scatter a few pieces of food down on the ground. This brings their focus back to the area immediately around you (**proximity**) and it brings their focus downwards (**calmness**).

However, if you have a dog where one of your struggles is that they are sniffing all the time (I mean their nose is glued to the ground), scatter feeding is not one to use too often.

If you have more than one dog, there are a few extra things to think about. Are they on different diets? Do you need to monitor the different amounts they eat? Or is it not safe for them to eat in the same area together? You could do separate scatter feeds in different places. Think about rooms you can use, your outside spaces etc. Can you do it at different times of day for each dog? There is a way to get around every challenge.

Have you got tall dogs and you use raised bowls? If you don't think they'll be comfortable being down so low, you could limit the amount of scatter feeding you do or place the food on a series of slightly higher up surfaces. Boxes inside? Upturned plant pots in the garden? Be creative!

If you feed a raw diet there are some things you can do to scatter feed. Look at freeze-dried or air-dried foods that you're happy with. Or dehydrate in small balls or use a 'pyramid' pan. You can also get free-flow frozen mince. You can scatter outside if that works for you or on a towel that you can throw in the washing machine afterwards.

Lick mats

Lick mats are a wonderful invention!

A lick mat is a textured feeding mat. They're normally made of silicone or rubber, and some are dishwasher safe (thank goodness!). Some have grids, some have bobbles and patterns, some are flat, some are bowls. Some have suckers on the back so that you can attach them to vertical surfaces.

If you want to see the ones I use (and I have a drawer full!) visit www. puptalk.co.uk and look at the links in *Useful Stuff*.

Licking is a very calming thing for dogs to do - so a daily lick mat is an easy and effective way to increase calmness in their day. You can use anything you like that is spreadable on the lick mat. Their wet food, raw food, natural yoghurt, coconut oil, mashed vegetables or fruit they like (sweet potato, carrot, apple and banana are often popular), dog-safe peanut butter, squeezy cheese, dog-safe pate. The list is endless – experiment!

If your pup is on any kind of restricted diet, you can moisten their dry food and spread that on. Remember to introduce any new food in small quantities to see how they like it and their tummies cope with it.

Great times and uses for lick mats:

- Got visitors coming round? Get a lick mat ready with something really tasty to put down just before people arrive (get them to text you when they're outside to set up their arrival for calmness).
- Use it for any distracting time in your household – meal times, when the post is due, getting ready to go out, noisy TV programmes?
- If your dog is pestering you to play or mouthing you. Telling them 'No!' might interrupt the behaviour but then what do they do? We can teach them to <u>choose</u> a different behaviour, like giving them a calming lick mat.
- I love giving Bodie a lick mat <u>before</u> we go out for a walk. It helps him start the walk in a calmer state.
- It can be a great way to start their whole day off. What they do first things can set the mood for the rest of the day.
- It's another great activity to grow your dog's **independence**. Pop the lick mat down in their crate or another room and leave them to it. You might need to build up this distance and duration slowly if they are anxious about being alone and out of sight of you.
- Pair it with times they find stressful. Don't just use it when fireworks are going off. It will probably be too much for them if they're scared of loud noises. But you can build up their confidence with noise by giving them a lick mat and playing noises quietly then build up the volumes levels over time.

I used to use lick mats 2-3 times a day for the first year with Bodie. They are such an effective calming tool (and they helped Ash and I stay calmer too!).

If your dog is happy getting stuck into lick mats, you can freeze them once you've topped them. This can make them last longer. If your dog likes to chew the lick mat, pop it down, supervise them, and take it away as soon as the lick mat is more interesting than what you've put on it.

Meaty bones

Meaty bones can be a really tasty treat to keep your dog busy for quite a while; chewing and gnawing are lovely calming activities.

I love a raw bone for Bodie; I think it helps to keep his teeth naturally clean. I give him 1-2 a week depending on the size of them (my lovely local butcher will save them for me and cut them up smaller if I need him to).

People ask me about the size and types of bones. It is a personal thing, and you need to decide what feels right for your dog. I'm not a massive fan of marrow bones - as much as Bodie loves them. I find the marrow centre gives him a runny tummy. You can refill them with your own fillings though once they've had the marrow out of them.

I give Bodie raw frozen chicken carcasses. Raw chicken is fine for a lot of dogs. The raw bones are quite flexible, and many dogs' jaws will cope just fine. Chicken necks or wings can be good for smaller dogs.

When people ask me about being worried about things our dogs eat, remember, quite a few of them eat poo! They do have very different stomachs compared to ours. They have much higher levels of acid to break down their food. We grind our food up with saliva to help extract the nutrients. The dog's stomach does that job for them. They don't have teeth to grind up food, they chomp, gulp it down, and let the stomach do its job.

This doesn't apply to non-edible things. You do need to watch out for long fibres, fabrics (from say toys or clothing) and rocks – these can't be broken down by the stomach and can cause dangerous blockages. Do avoid giving dogs cooked bones; these become brittle when cooked and are more likely to splinter.

If your dog has powerful jaws, bones can be given to your dog frozen to last longer. A lot of dogs will bury a bone first or hide the chew in their bed or cover it with your lovely rug. Bodie buries his in the compost heap. It's a natural instinct. It's throwback behaviour to their grey wolf and wild dog ancestors when food wasn't always plentiful. Burying it would preserve it if they didn't need to eat it straight away. So they can want to stash away something big or extra tasty like a bone.

I find if I give Bodie a hairy rabbit ear (or 'furry crisp' as we call them), he'll happily chomp on it straight away (see the section coming up on long-lasting chews). If I give him something larger like a cow's ear or a bone, he'll nearly always bury it. Well, that's after running around the garden at least 15 times before deciding where the best place to bury it is!

After a good chew on a bone, Bodie will normally take himself off for a nap. It's exhausting!

Do keep an eye on bones. Get rid of them before they are small enough to be a choking hazard. Watch for any cracks, sharp or jagged bits.

Giving your dog bones is a personal choice. Dogs can chip and break teeth on them. If you have any concerns, have a chat with your vet.

There is old training advice that used to encourage you to take a bone (or something tasty) off your dog part way through them eating it. To make sure they 'knew you were in charge'. This is a very bad idea. If your dog is prone to resource guarding, it is will probably make it worse and if your dog didn't resource guard before, they might start.

If you took a bar of chocolate off me halfway through, I would not be happy about it. I would probably tell you off. It would make me want to take it away somewhere quiet and not to trust you if you came near me when I had chocolate in the future. However, if you offered me something else tasty, in exchange for what I already had, I would learn that it's OK to let go because there is something equally good on offer. You would gain my trust.

Now of course I'm not saying give your dog chocolate. That would be dangerous. But it was the best example I could think of to illustrate the point.

There are great games to help dogs that resource guard and to teach all dogs that they can trust us. Taking a bone off them partway through is not one of them. Please also make sure that dogs are given plenty of space to enjoy a high-value treat. Even walking past them can be too much for some dogs. This is especially important for children and visitors who might not be aware your dog has something really tasty.

It's another great chance to give them some space (time in a crate, pen, garden, separate room) and grow their sense of **independence**.

Scent work

Getting our dogs to use their nose is a fabulous activity for every dog! A huge part of their brain is used in processing smells. As dogs evolved, they needed an amazing sense of smell to find food, know which other animals and dogs had been in the area, to mate, to survive.

'Olfaction' is simply the action of smelling. It's a massive part of how our dogs process the world around them. Dogs have a basic instinct to search and investigate.

They can 'see' the world through the smells around them; it's so hard for us to comprehend the amount of information they can gather with this sense.

For most of us, our primary sense is sight; for all of us lucky enough to have our sight, imagine if we were made to wear a blindfold most of the time. That's what we're doing by stopping our dogs from sniffing.

And we're not just talking about dogs that are 'scenting' breeds, like Bloodhounds, Spaniels and Dachshunds. All breeds and types of dogs use their nose all the time and because so much of their brains are engaged, it's a very rewarding and tiring activity. Win-win!

So if you've got a flat-faced (brachycephalic) dog, don't skip ahead! Honestly, unless your dog has no nose - cue a terrible cracker joke. Every dog, with any kind of sense of smell, can get something out of using its nose more.

Scent games are brilliant for dogs of all ages. Puppies can recognise scent before they are born. That's how they find where their mother's milk is coming from before they've even opened their eyes. It's never too early to start scent games.

In older dogs, their other senses of sight and hearing often diminish with age. But they rarely completely lose their sense of smell. It's a fabulous way to enrich an older dog's later years - it will help to keep their brain active – use it or lose it!

It's also a wonderful way to build up your relationship with them. When you're playing a scenting game that they love, the sniffing is very rewarding for them. They also associate the rewarding feelings with you. Please don't think 'scent work' is complicated. Even simple scatter feeding is really using our dogs' noses.

Scenting games are brilliant for dogs that:

- Struggle to be calm.
- Get over-excited.
- Struggle to switch off.
- Have so much energy, you cannot tire them out on a traditional 'walk'.
- Love to sniff! You can channel their sniffing skills rather them dragging you along on a walk.
- Are nervous or reactive to other dogs/people/the environment etc. – scenting can be fabulous to help build confidence and change where their focus is.
- Are on any kind of restricted exercise – crate rest, lead walks only or when you're unable to take them out.

- Dogs that struggle to be left alone (separation anxiety and other issues).
- Senior dogs – mental decline (canine cognitive dysfunction) is quite common in older dogs.

Let's look at some of these a little more.

My dog gets so over-excited and rarely switches off

Using their noses more is one of the most brilliant ways to help dogs that don't naturally know how to be calm. It requires a little focus and concentration on their part and generally, a dog that is sniffing on the ground can't be jumping up and down at you or your visitors at the same time!

Scent games are more tiring than chasing around a field after another dog or a ball but with the bonus of helping them learn a calm activity, rather than getting more and more over-excited and filling up their bucket.

My dog won't stop sniffing

If you've got a very nose-focused dog, you might be thinking you don't want to encourage them to sniff even more. "Surely, they'll just get worse?"

In fact, it's the opposite. Giving them structured activities, and even putting sniffing on a cue, can give them an outlet so that when you're not playing scent games you can get more focus on you rather than every interesting blade of grass!

Nervous and reactive dogs

If you can't walk your dog without them reacting negatively to other dogs (or other triggers), using their sense of smell can do amazing things.

Once you have taught your dog a simple scent game, it can boost their confidence and focus, as well as growing the relationship between you and your dog. Using scent games in training with a reactive dog can have significant positive impacts on their behaviour.

If you want a little science behind it, the dopamine receptors in a dog's brain are key to reducing anxiety. They help focus attention and promote feelings of satisfaction. Studies have shown that sniffing reduces a dog's pulse rate, even when they are physically active, as the intensity of sniffing increases, so their pulse rate lowers.

I had the pleasure of recording a podcast with Louise Wilson, Founder of the Conservation K9 Consultancy. Her work includes training specialist detection dogs for wildlife monitoring and detection work. Her personal pack of 10 dogs are all ex-rescue dogs that came to her with some significant behaviour problems; scent work has changed their lives. You can listen to this episode by searching for Pup Talk The Podcast episode #23 on iTunes, Spotify, or your usual podcast platform.

Dogs that struggle to be left alone (separation anxiety and other issues)

For dogs that struggle with **independence** (being happy on their own), scent work can be a really useful tool.

Right from the basics of laying a **food trail**, leading them away from you or sending them away from you to find a toy. Or a **scatter feed** in the garden, or another room to you.

If you are looking for a calming activity that doesn't involve food, you can scatter some dog-safe herbs or spices for some great enrichment.

Over time, you can grow the distance and visual barriers between you, which are crucial parts of helping a dog learn **independence** from you.

Senior dogs (approx. 7+ years old, depending on breed / size)

Mental decline (canine cognitive dysfunction) is quite common in older dogs.

In some older dogs, you might start to notice that they get a bit disorientated, stare at walls, get lost in your garden, stand in the wrong place to go out into the garden. Toileting accidents can start to happen and they can get grumpy, or worse, with other dogs when they used to be fine.

They might start barking more. They can start waking in the middle of the night for no apparent reason. They might be less engaged with you or get more clingy with you.

Scent games can play a wonderful role in helping older dogs live a happy life for as long as possible. Even when their eyesight and hearing deteriorate, generally their sense of smell is the last to diminish. Playing scent games, alongside a fully enriched life, can also help to slow down the rate of mental and physical decline.

Creating **food trails** over low or different textured objects can assist with gentle movement and maintaining mobility. Scent games can be part of a plan of physical therapies. You might want to investigate swimming or underwater treadmills for low impact exercise. Massage with appropriate aromatherapy products can be great, incorporating the senses of touch and smell.

Simple scent games

So you know one scent game already – **scatter feeding**. The easiest place to start.

You can buy a **snuffle mat** or make your own if you have quite a lot of patience. I like the lazy version of scattering some of their dinner on a dog towel (we all have designated dog towels, don't we?) and then grab the centre with splayed fingers and rotate your hand around. You make a large 'swirl' with food hiding in the folds of the towel.

You can release them to it (from a wait, a stay or another room) and leave them to snuffle around to find their dinner. If your dog is new to this, you might need to stay and encourage them with a cue like 'find it' and some finger-pointing to find the food and help them understand what the game is. I find a few tastier, smellier pieces of food mixed with daily dry food can work well.

You can also buy a cheap little shaggy rug or a fringed mop head for a snuffle mat. Anything they can snuffle the food out of will work. Just make sure they don't chew and ingest (swallow) any of the material.

There's another version of this which I call the 'Swiss roll' tea towel. Scatter some food on a towel where you would spread the jam on a sponge for a Swiss roll (no I've never made a real one but I do love watching the Great British Bake-Off). Then roll it up and pop it on the floor. If you've got a dog that likes to grab and shake the towel to get the food out – don't worry. They use their brain to work out how they want to get to the food and they create themselves a little self-scatter feed.

There is never a wrong way to play a game. Just make sure to pick the towel or mat up if there is any chewing, tearing, or humping! Anything you'd rather they didn't do.

Sniffing out and working for each piece of food is so much more natural than finding food in a bowl.

Dogs that are not that 'foodie' can get much more interested in their food once they get used to 'working' for it.

So even if your household is frantic first thing in the morning, and you have absolutely no time, you can do a **scatter feed** or a **homemade snuffle towel** in 30 seconds and then get on with everything else you need to do. It probably takes less time for you to do this than it does to stop your dog from getting under your feet while you're trying to get ready.

For puppies, or any dogs new to scenting games, you can create a **scent path**. It's like scatter feeding but, in a line, (straight or curving). Start by placing the food 5–15cm apart, then space the food out a little more as they get better at it. This is a great game to build **confidence** and grow **independence** as they are busy and choose to move away from you. Start the food trails on a hard surface (indoors or outdoors) and then build up the difficulty on different surfaces like grass or stones or a rug.

The **Coin indication game** is a great way to get your dog to indicate a specific object to you.

You can use an object like a coin, pop it on the floor and drop food on and closely around the coin. You're looking for focus on the coin. You can stroke them while they're focusing downwards at the coin/food. This can be your signal for them to keep going.

It can help the dog stay focused downwards if you can crouch down to start with, then you can start to stand up when they understand the game is to focus on the coin. You can also cue a 'down' so that the down becomes the indication for finding the object.

'Reset' them every so often by throwing a piece of food away for them to follow and start again if they come back to you (telling you they want to carry on the game).

You can simply **hide a favourite toy** and encourage them to 'go find it' (or the toy's name if they know it). Go and find it together until you know they can happily find it themselves.

You can make walks so much more tiring and rewarding by adding in games that use their sense of smell. I will toss a few treats into an area where I am happy for Bodie to sniff about and release him to this space with a 'go sniff!' cue.

Noise box is another great game that uses their nose. You'll find that in Chapter 12.

With any scenting game, if they are looking to you for help, or losing interest, they are finding it too difficult. Make it easier for them to keep it fun and interesting. There are lots of specific scent training classes, courses and workshops you can attend if you want to explore what your dog's incredible nose can do. It's mentally and physically tiring so a great way to give our dogs stimulation and exercise without even leaving the house.

When we're talking about concepts that are supercharged with any sniffing games, we are working on **calmness**, **confidence**, **optimism** and **independence**. All great skills for every dog to have.

Slow Feeder 'Bowls' / Puzzle Feeders / Interactive Toys

There are lots of different types of slow feeder bowls and puzzle feeders that you can buy. They are all designed to slow down the speed that your dog eats their food. Or they have to work out some kind of puzzle to get the food.

I personally haven't bought any for Bodie because:

1. Many are made of plastic (and I've bought enough things that will end up in landfill sites at some point).
2. Once your dog has worked out the puzzle, they may get bored.
3. If they can't work out the puzzle, they may get frustrated or bored.
4. They're not cheap (and Bodie's food alone is £££!).
5. I can make my own for free from a loo roll inner, an egg box or milk carton (and any other objects that are going out with my recycling) and make them as easy or as tricky as my dog is ready for.
6. I use an old muffin tin with balls covering food in the holes for a puzzle feeder, or upside down for a slow feeder bowl.
7. It's more stuff for the over-full kitchen cupboards!

If you feed raw, I think a slow feeder bowl (or lick mat) can be a really useful thing for inside spaces where you don't want raw food all over the place. I tend to stuff a cow's hoof or trachea for a natural alternative and always give them to Bodie in the garden. But he will eat a raw-stuffed hoof in the snow so it might not work for all dogs! You can give them to your dog when they are in their crate or pen with a dog towel down for any mess. The towel can then go straight into the washing machine afterwards.

There are some lovely crafted wooden puzzle toys though. These could be great for a dog on crate rest/restricted movement. So if you like the idea of buying something, why not give these a try?

Filled Kongs / Kong Wobbler / Toppl / Treat Balls

Kongs are probably the most well-known canine enrichment toy. These are made from pretty durable rubber and they come in different sizes and durability. You can get small ones for puppies and small breeds, right up to extra large for big dogs and big chewers. They're not cheap but after two years of hard chewing from Bodie, our black Kongs only have a few dents in them (we freeze them, so he chews pretty hard on them). You can stuff them with all sorts of food. You can start easy by putting a few treats or their dry food in it and they'll fall out straight away. Or just smear a bit of dog-safe peanut butter and get them used to licking it.

Build up the difficulty if they enjoy it by 'buttering' the insides with something wet and sticky and then you can stick dry ingredients inside. The harder you pack it, the harder it is. Don't think challenging is always better. They can lose interest. Use their daily wet food, moistened kibble/dry food, natural yoghurt, dog-safe peanut butter, coconut oil, mashed fruit and veggies like sweet potato, carrot, banana, or apple. Anything they like!

Finish off the filling (large opening) with something super tasty like a little chicken/cheese/doggy peanut butter or have a tasty treat sticking out like dried sprats or a pizzle to get them interested in it. Yummy! Like a 99 ice cream with a Flake in it!

There are all sorts of different toys you can stuff for canine enrichment. Toppl, from West Paw, is another great one. They have a lifetime recycle policy at the time of writing, which I love.

The Kong Wobbler has been a good toy for Bodie. He wasn't into it for the first few months, but now and again we'd get it out. All of a sudden, he started pushing it over with his nose and paws and will happily make kibble fly all over the kitchen floor, making lots of noise! Great for **confidence** building and dogs that bark at noises.

Although these are often called 'treat' balls or treat dispensers, remember this can just be their normal daily food. All food in a day should be taken into consideration for their total calorie intake (Chapter 6 touches on avoiding weight gain).

For safety, I wouldn't leave a dog unsupervised with any canine enrichment toy. A frozen stuffed Kong can create a vacuum that their tongue could get stuck in. You can freeze them with a skewer or straw through the middle (that you remove before giving to them!). Freezing them makes them last longer and is great if your dog likes a challenge, or for teething puppies.

Along with keeping our dogs' brains occupied, some toys help with keeping teeth and gums healthy. I prefer toys that are too large rather than too small, to reduce the risk of a choking hazard. It's always a good idea to supervise them and throw away (or recycle) any toy that is showing signs of damage.

Long-Lasting Chews (Trachea, Hooves etc.)

Now some of these items are not great if you're a bit squeamish. I get that. But most dogs really enjoy them and, most importantly for me, chewing is a naturally calming activity. I always opt for natural, long-lasting chews over something manufactured. You are normally picking a single source protein, they're natural, no chemicals, no preservatives (look for ones that are air-dried) and no rawhide. A single-source protein (i.e. from one animal) makes it easier to exclude something if it doesn't agree with your dog.

The list of natural chews available for our dogs is now huge! This list is not exhaustive, but it might give you some ideas of new things to try:

- Pizzles – a classic chew, you can get different sizes.
- Chicken, turkey, and duck feet.
- Fish skins.
- Trachea – give them to your dog plain, or they're great for stuffing.
- Chicken, duck, and goose necks.
- Rabbits ears – with or without fur. With natural fibre, it's great as a natural de-wormer (I do still give Bodie a prescription worming medication, although there are other options).
- Lamb, pig, cow, goat, and buffalo ears (these range from quite small to really big, and hairy or non-hairy).
- Cow and buffalo tails.
- Chicken and duck wings.
- Hooves – a great natural chew, can also be stuffed and frozen for an even longer-lasting chew. They can also be made more 'interesting' if you need to with a light spread of dog-safe peanut butter or coconut oil and frozen.
- Gullet sticks (oesophagus muscle).
- Rabbit pelts and feet.
- Hairy beef scalp.
- Buffalo skin, hairy cow, and venison skin.
- Bull's testes (erm, yep! Surprisingly small, Bodie loved them).
- Beef and lamb muscle, beef tendon.
- Beef cheek.
- Lamb and buffalo lung.
- Dried liver pieces and dried tripe.

- Lamb and venison legs.
- Pig snouts and cow noses.
- Chicken hearts.
- Dried prawns.
- Paddywack (cow neck ligament).
- Antler, cow, and buffalo horn.
- Ostrich bone.
- Coffeewood, olivewood chew sticks and chewroots.
- The list could go on!

Lots of these are widely available in local pet shops, online etc. There are links to suppliers I know and love at the back of this book if you need any sources.

Except for the wood chews, this list above is all very meaty (and a little fishy). You can get vegetable alternatives – sweet potato chews are great and fairly easy to make yourself.

Bodie is a meat lover but will sometimes chew on a Rice Bone. Beyond that, he's not very interested in anything fruit or vegetable-based. But do try things with your dog; they are all different. For some dogs, a carrot will be the best treat ever. My mum's dog Lucy will go crazy for a stick of carrot and one of my clients found out by accident that her dog loved the hard stalk centre from a cabbage. They all have different tastes!

You may have tried a Yak milk chew – Bodie likes them, but they don't last him very long. You can microwave them when they get smaller to puff them up and make them bigger again. They're made with yak and cow's milk and lime juice and salt. You can make them yourself if you like to try new things! Surely there will be a Doggy Bake-Off series one day?

I love a varied diet for dogs, but I am not a nutritionist. Please do your research and make sure you are picking items that are suitable for the breed/size of your dog. Some chews are great for joint health, some are lower in fat.

Some vets will advise you to stay away from very hard chews like antlers due to the risk of breaking teeth. Antlers are fairly unlikely to split or splinter but it can happen. For my dog, I think hard chews are important to help keep his teeth clean naturally. But please do what is right for your dog.

Puppies who are teething may alternate between loving hard chews and not wanting them as they go through the teething phase. Have different densities and textures for them.

Older dogs, or any dogs with problems with their teeth and gums, may struggle with harder chews.

With anything new, give them a small amount first to see how they get on with it. Some bigger chews can be cut up with sturdy kitchen scissors (I may have used a branch saw from the shed for bigger items but I'm not recommending this for obvious health and safety reasons!). Maybe avoid a multipack until you've found out if they like something and if it agrees with them. You can visit my website www.puptalk.co.uk if you need any more ideas.

Some dogs can get over-excited with some high-value chews and foods. If this is an issue, use lower value ones, while you're working on growing their **calmness** skills.

As with bones, dogs will often run around (sometimes crying a little) looking for a place to bury something for another time. Now there isn't a feast and famine going on for most of our dogs but this seems to happen if the item is new or highly valued by them (it could be your slipper!). Or it could be that they're not hungry enough for it yet and want to stash it away for later when they think no one is going to disturb them.

So any of these prize items could end up in your flower bed, under their blanket or your duvet! If this is a problem, you can switch to smaller chews. As covered in the section on meaty bones, I would never recommend trying to take a high value treat off your dog. If you have any concerns about resource guarding, I strongly recommend you consult with a professional.

Please note, anything can be a choking hazard. If you are in any doubt, do not leave chews lying around for your dog.

Massage and calm stroking

Although not passive on your part, I do include calming stroking and massage here. If your dog enjoys physical contact this can be a lovely calming activity.

If your pup is mouthing you while you stroke them, perhaps you can give them a soft toy to hold in their mouth. Or a harder textured chew like a Nylabone. If they're not teething puppies, it may be that they just like to hold something in their mouths. Either way, it will discourage them from trying to chew on your fingers.

Not all dogs enjoy being stroked though; they may just tolerate it. Your dog's body language is something to learn so that you can read their signals as to whether this is something they enjoy or not.

What is right for your dog?

With all of the activities in this section, get to know what is right for your dog and decide what is safe for them. Please do your research for your type of dog and make an informed decision.

When we are redirecting them from the behaviour that we don't like, don't think that we are rewarding them so that they'll do more of it. Try to time the giving of the passive calming activity with a moment of calmness (even just a nano-second of slightly less crazy behaviour). Over time they will start to choose calmer behaviour more of the time. But it does take consistency and some time.

2. The calmness protocol – things you can do to help grow calmness

The second part of the calmness wheel is the **calmness protocol**. This might sound fancy, but it is just a simple principle - you get more of what you reward. So we want to reward exactly the right things, at the right time.

There are lots of different ways we can do this.

Reward nothing and reward good choices

The first game is simply to **reward nothing**. How do I do that? When you see your dog or puppy doing nothing at all, that is a great opportunity to use some of their daily food allowance and just pop a piece down in front of them.

We tend to ignore our dogs when they're not doing anything. It's easy to think,

> *"Thank goodness, the dog is quiet for a few minutes, I'm going to get on with (insert any number of things from your lengthy to-do list)."*

But this is a perfect time to spot them not doing anything and reward it. We're not going crazy with praise, just putting a piece of food down calmly in front of them as you walk past. No fuss.

In the same way, you can **reward good choices**. So, if your dog is sitting down nice and calmly and perhaps somebody got up and went to the kitchen. If normally, your dog might get up and follow, if they stayed still on one occasion - that is a great choice. Pop a piece of food down calmly for them.

You can 'play' **reward nothing** and **reward good choices** at any point in the day.

I suggest having some of your dog's daily food to hand wherever you are, in the lounge, in the bedroom, in the kitchen, in the bathroom, in your pocket when you are out. It means you're never far from some food to be able to 'capture' and reward those moments of calm.

I'll talk you through my logistics of having food in the right place at the right time in Chapter 6 – Ditch the bowl. You don't want to have to run off to the kitchen to grab some food only to have missed the moment as they follow you to see what you're doing. This is where precise timing really makes a difference. The reward needs to be delivered quickly and calmly.

Your dog will work out that when they are calm, they get good things. So it's a really good deal for them to do these things more often. You really can't use this strategy too much. Brief the whole family on how this game works.

Now **ninja feeding** takes **reward nothing** to a whole new level. This can be easy, or it can be difficult, to virtually impossible. It depends on how vigilant your dog is and how deeply they sleep.

This game involves putting a piece of food down in front of their nose, while your pup is fast asleep. Hopefully, they don't wake up as you're approaching like a super stealth ninja in your bare feet or socks.

If your dog opens one eye, that's fine. If they wake up and eat the food straight away that's also fine. You might manage the full ninja feed by the food being there in front of their nose waiting for them when they wake up. This is the ultimate **reward nothing**!

There is no right or wrong way for this one. It doesn't matter if they spot you approaching. Or when they open that one eye and they see a piece of chicken or kibble in front of their nose, most of them will just eat it and settle back down again. It is all promoting that positive cycle of calmness. They will learn to settle and switch off more easily.

Don't think that you are disturbing the **calmness** (or perhaps sleep) with this game. It's the opposite. Remember that that you get more of what you reward.

I think this can be a lovely game for children to be involved with and, in my experience, they love it too. Just a word of caution. With anyone (adults and kids) do make sure that a sleeping dog is not 'hassled' in their crate or bed. This is about placing a piece of food quietly in front of their nose and retreating. No stroking or crowding them at all. Please be confident that your dog is fine with being approached when they are resting or asleep. This is one to supervise and make sure everyone is playing it safely and happily.

If you have any concerns about how your dog would react if approached when sleeping, please use common sense to know what's going to work for your dog.

Timing is key – reward when they're calm

Let's stop for a moment to talk about the timing of the rewards. The aim is to deliver the reward when they are calm. Now depending on the kind of puppy or dog you've got these opportunities to reward might be nanoseconds! If you have got a very busy dog, you are going to have to capture the **relative moments of calm**. If you have got a dog that will sit and be still for a second or more, fabulous. You are going to be able to reward those moments of calm fairly easily.

However, you may well be here because you have got a crazy puppy on your hands, and there are not many parts of the day when you would describe them as calm. But spot the little micro-moments when they are relatively calm and time your reward with that. Again, you will get more of what you reward. Those moments of calm should grow ever so slightly, little by little. Keep doing it as this does work in time.

Time feeding with distractions

It's helpful to time feeding with distractions as much as you can. Make a list now of the things that your pup finds difficult. It could be a visitor, or recycling/bin day, or when a neighbour is cutting the lawn.

If your dog is anything like mine, it could be a squirrel running along the fence in the back garden, which they seem to do most first thing in the morning.

Where you can, time calm feeding with those distractions on your list. This will help your dog learn these distractions as 'none of their business'. Nothing to be worried about or excited by. We'll also look at a game later in this book called DMT (in Chapter 12) where I will specifically teach you how to do this.

Crate time can be a great thing and you can pair crate time with any of the passive calming activities we've covered. Things like a stuffed Kong, or a long-lasting chew, are an amazing thing to use for some relaxing crate time. Or it could be relaxing in another room or their bed or puppy pen.

3. Rest – you may be surprised but not all dogs know how to rest

It might seem strange, but some dogs are not good at resting and sleeping.

Let's look at puppies first.

Puppies can get a lot like over-tired children. They don't want to miss out on anything and they often don't know how to switch off and rest when they need to. The more tired they get, the worse they get. This is not a good cycle and will quickly have you frazzled and wondering why on earth you thought getting a puppy would be a good idea!

You might notice the biting, barking and jumping getting worse later in the day. Or it builds up after an exciting walk, a vigorous play session, or some time at doggy day-care. Remember that little puppy bucket – it over-flows very easily.

Add into that the phase of teething and mouth pain disturbing their sleep and then developing hormones for both sexes. It's no wonder they're not always able to rest when they need to.

Adult dogs can also struggle to switch off and rest. It could be that they are a naturally busy breed, always seeming to be on the go. Some breeds are designed to notice everything, like herding breeds (this is called hypervigilance).

As dogs age, they can also struggle to sleep as well.

It could be that your dog's environment is very busy, with lots of people moving around, making noise, and affecting their ability to sleep. Or there are noises and movements outside the home that they struggle to detach from.

It could be learned behaviours, that have increased over time. Or it could just be their natural personality.

Sleeping beauty

Rest is the third part of the calmness wheel, and it is just as important as the other two (passive calming and the calmness protocol) and we are talking about good quality rest. It doesn't always have to be sleep.

Do you ever stop to watch how well your dog rests and sleeps? You could keep a simple diary to note the hours they're either:

1. High energy.
2. Medium energy.
3. Low energy (resting or sleeping).

Add up the totals per day and then you can come back to this in weeks to come to see how things are progressing.

Puppies in particular need a lot of sleep. At 8-12 weeks of age, they could be sleeping/resting for 18-20 hours a day. Their brains have got a lot of developing to do and it's hard work. But all puppies are different. Like us, especially children, if we are tired, we are more likely to be cranky and tetchy and make bad decisions. It is just the same with puppies and also adult dogs.

It's useful to think about where your dog spends most of its time resting and sleeping. Where is their bed or crate? Is it tucked out of the way, or it is in a thoroughfare where people are walking past them all the time?

Do they have a separate room where they can rest more easily? Some dogs will need encouragement to rest slightly further away from the busier parts of the house. A lot of our homes are open plan and although the dog looks like they are sleeping, it may well be that their rest is not as good quality as it could be.

You might want to think about where they are sleeping most of the time and move this spot into a quieter location if you can. Crates and pens are fantastic at helping our dogs learn to rest. Personally, I would never have a situation where a puppy or a dog is shut in a crate, a pen or a room against their will. 'Leaving them to cry it out'. What we want to do is create a positive association with the quiet space. We can do this by using passive calming activities to make it a really good experience for them. So, a tasty lick mat or a nice chew or bone is put into their space with them.

We want them to look forward to these 'timeouts'.

Separate rooms are good for adult dogs as well. I use a bedroom for Bodie when we want to give him some timeout. We will just shut the bedroom door to give him a little peace and quiet away from the noise of us working online or the TV. He now seeks out this space on his own.

Don't forget you can use rooms like bathrooms and utility rooms if that works for you.

To be very clear - this is not a punishment. This is creating a calm space and encourages them to switch off and rest.

Boundary games are something that we are going to talk about in Chapter 12. But if you have already done any boundary/place games, if you have got a dog that is happy on their boundary or bed, this is another great place for rest.

Crates and crying

When you are using crates, pens, or another room this is absolutely not 'lock them in and leave them to cry it out.'

There are different types of barking, whining, and crying. You need to get to know the difference with your dog. Do they sound stressed and anxious, - *don't leave me alone!* - this can be escalating, relentless, and sounds genuinely distressed. Perhaps a sharp bark at repeated at intervals, or whining. Even if this sounds like they are looking for attention, it is still coming from a dog who is experiencing unpleasant emotions. Barking in a crate or pen can often be due to overexcitement, covering it with a light cover can help because you are just giving them a gentle visual barrier to help them settle down.

Whatever the reason they are not settling down in this space, we need to help them learn that this time is enjoyable. Make sure that you are not forcing them into something that they are not yet comfortable with. If you invest a little time and some high-value rewards, you can create a dog that is happy to settle on its own. This will be invaluable in later life. They need to see this place as somewhere that they enjoy and learn to be calm and settled.

Please note: If the puppy or dog is genuinely distressed about being on their own in any space, I strongly recommend getting professional help.

More than one dog – double trouble?

If you have more than one dog in your home, you have a 'multi-dog household.'

When we look at our dogs' buckets in a multi-dog household, each dog has their own bucket. But there is also a household bucket. Everything can get multiplied and magnified and this can affect their ability to rest properly. You might have one dog who is pretty good at switching off and taking itself off for a sleep. Then you have another dog who gets over-excited or stressed by noises outside the home, or can't stop following you around the home.

The dog that has the smaller bucket will be affecting (filling up) the bucket of the more chilled out dog. You can use 'gated communities' to help your dogs each get the rest they need. This means if you've got a young puppy, perhaps, and an older dog, it is quite likely that the older dog might get a little bit frustrated and tired with an over-exuberant puppy.

You can use baby gates to separate rooms without having all the doors shut. You can have the puppy or another dog in their crate or pen. Or you can have them in separate rooms. We want to try and make sure that one dog is not affecting the quality of the rest of the other dogs.

When one dog is calm and the other is not, the calm dog is being affected by the dog that is not so calm and things can escalate. It is worth just thinking about where your dogs can get some good quality rest. What can you do to try and make that better quality? It will help any behaviour struggles.

The calmness wheel

If you need a reminder of the three parts of the calmness wheel, this graphic will help.

Passive Calming
- Scatter feeding
- Lick mats
- Meaty bones
- Scenting
- Puzzle feeders
- Filled Kongs
- Treat balls
- Dehydrated treats
- Filled trachea/hooves

  Rest
  - Rooms
  - Crates / pens
  - Boundaries for experienced dogs
  - Gated communities for multi-dog households

Calmness Protocol
- Reward nothing
- Reward good choices
- Ninja feeding
- Reward when calm
- Time feeding with distractions
- Crate time with passive calming activity

6

IT'S TIME TO GET DITCHING

What we know about our dogs and how their brains work has grown so much in recent years and it will keep growing. There are two 'frameworks' from Absolute Dogs that are useful to cover here. They both play a part in helping us to shape our dogs' behaviours.

Ditch the bowl

The first framework that I want to cover is 'ditch the bowl.' If you're not already doing it, I know that might seem daft. But I promise you not using a bowl (or a plate!) to feed your dog will change you and your pup's life.

So, why on earth would you not use a food bowl?

Dogs didn't evolve finding nice shiny bowls of delicious food in the corners of our kitchens. They evolved mostly scavenging for scraps around human encampments. They had to work for it.

If you like a geeky term, we are talking about animals that are contra freeloaders. They like to work for their food - they are genetically programmed to forage and hunt – and find it rewarding. That's how their ancestors would have survived.

Dopamine (a feel-good hormone) is released when searching for (anticipating) rather than eating the food. Given the choice between food freely available and food they have to work for, the food tastes better when they work for it.

I regularly see clients who say "My dog doesn't really like their dry kibble. I have to mix it with wet food to get them to eat it." Once we start playing the right games with their food, they suddenly start to happily eat each piece of kibble.

The number one reason for me to ditch the bowl is that there is so much value in the food you give your pup. It seems such a shame to 'waste it' by just giving it to them in a bowl. Yes, your dog will get the nutrition, but that's all. It's arguably the biggest single thing you can do to increase the bond between you and your pup. There's so much you can do with it to help all sorts of training and relationship building.

It increases the bond between you and your pup; even just hand feeding them around the home builds that relationship. Measure out their daily allowance and the whole family can get involved without over or under-feeding.

Would your life be easier if your pup was calmer and more focused on you when you were out walking? Imagine the value your pup would see in being by your side when you're out walking if they're calm before you go out and that's where they get fed their food as you're out on your walk.

If you play training games, or take your pup out walking, when they're hungry, i.e. before they've eaten, they will be much more motivated to work with you. Imagine being able to reward your dog and reinforce good choices with their normal daily food, and not just 'treats'.

Moment by moment, your dog is making choices as to what they do. Some choices are ones that we don't want – it might be pulling in the lead, barking, or lunging at another dog.

Most of these choices are instinctual. Instinctively our dog is worried; this was very useful for survival thousands of years ago or our dogs' ancestors were bred to pull. The more they do something, the more normal it feels, the better they get at it.

The opposite of this picture is, if you use your food to reward good choices, you're creating new habits. "When I see a distraction, I look at my mum and I get a reward." So, don't be afraid to use food for rewards. This is not bribery. Even if you love your job, would you go to work forever if you weren't getting paid?

Yes, you can use toys, touch, and praise as rewards as well. The more options you have for rewarding your dog, the easier it is to reinforce the good behaviours that you want more of. You can reward with praise if you haven't got any food on you. But you need to have taught the behaviours with rewards first.

Are you thinking about the reasons why ditching the bowl isn't going to work for you and your dog? Perhaps...

1. I haven't got time.
2. I don't want to carry around food with me forever.
3. I feed raw.
4. They'll start scavenging for food all over the place.
5. My dog isn't a foodie dog.

Let's look at these.

1. I haven't got time

It doesn't need to take any extra time. Rather than putting their dry food in a bowl, you can scatter it on the ground or scatter it into a snuffle mat or a box with a few objects in it.Or, put some of their dry food in a bag and take it with you when you take your dog out. You can play a few games, using their breakfast or dinner, and before you know you've used up all of their meal.

You can play a 2-minute game, while you're waiting for the kettle to boil, or there's an ad break on. Just use some of their daily food allowance.

Check out all of the easy ideas in Chapter 5.

2. I don't want to carry around food with me forever

Here's the secret - you won't need to carry around their food forever, but you will for a while. Food is the best tool that we have to train them and to help them to make great choices. Every single piece of food is an opportunity to say, "you did a great job, right there!" And again. And again.

If you can help them learn to make great choices, everything else gets easier. You will have more time. You won't have to be constantly telling your dog what you want them to do or stop them from doing things you don't want them to do!

3. I feed raw

There are lots of ways to ditch the bowl, even if you feed raw. You can use raw on lick mats, to stuff Kongs and hooves etc. (and freeze them if your dog likes more of a challenge). Look at the **passive calming** ideas in Chapter 5.

You can also get reusable squeezy tubes to deliver raw when you are on the go, without the mess. Plus you can use dehydrated and air-dried foods for games when you're out and about.

4. They'll start scavenging for food all over the place

Because we're giving our dogs a specific outlet to search for or work for their food, they are less likely to be searching out food all the time. You are giving their natural dog instincts an outlet. You can also put anything on a cue when it's time to have a scatter feed for instance.

5. But my dog isn't a foodie dog

Some dogs will happily eat anything you give them. Some dogs are very fussy. Dogs that happily work for their food make training and helping any behaviours much easier. The good news is that even dogs that are not that into their food, can become a lot more interested in food.

You can grow a foodie dog. The key is seeing what they enjoy doing when they are playing and just being themselves. Do they like to catch and jump? Do they like to chase things down or pounce on things? Do they like contact with you? All of this gives us clues as to how we can play games with their food that tap into their natural instincts and loves.

Why not try ditching the bowl, even for just one meal a day. If you're new to this idea, build up the amount of your dog's daily food that doesn't go into a bowl over time. You can start with as little as 25%, and that might be giving them a lick mat or a long-lasting chew instead of some of their usual food.

You can start small and build on it and once you start seeing the power of what ditching the bowl can do, I think you'll want to explore it more.

Ditch the routine

Do you have a dog that barks when you're getting ready to go for a walk? Or that whines when you're in the car? Or that goes 'on strike' when you're trying to head out of a park and just puts the brakes on? I grew up with 'old school' dog trainers on TV and I remember hearing about how it's good for dogs to have a routine. Basically – 'they know what's coming and when, and this is good for them.' We now know this isn't the case.

The problem is that routine creates a puppy or dog that struggles to be **flexible**. If they don't get fed or walked at the time they are used to, it means anticipation builds up and they can get frustrated or they get anxious or over-excited about what they know is coming. This can lead to barking, chewing, or other destructive or disruptive behaviours. Or when you do take them out walking, perhaps they are lunging at people or barking at other dogs, or just not able to walk calmly on the lead beside you.

A **flexible** pup is a good thing; you can't always do the same things at the same time - life gets in the way. Plus, how much easier is it to have a pup that isn't controlling the household timetable. You've probably got enough things to deal with in life without a demanding dog as well.

Recently I was chatting to a lady with two Bassett Hounds (when out walking our dogs we always end up talking to other dog people don't we?). She told me at 6pm her dogs would woof like crazy if she didn't have their food out on time and those are big barks! But it doesn't have to be like that.

Dogs are excellent at predicting what's about to happen; this creates anticipation. It might be something exciting that they're looking forward to but it also might be something that they find stressful (and we might not even be aware of this). Either way, too much anticipation isn't a good thing.

If your pup is prone to pulling on the lead, barking at squirrels, reacting to other dogs or joggers, or is a bit hit and miss with their recall (or any other behaviour that you'd rather they didn't do), their state of anticipation and increased arousal is likely to be a factor.

If you can reduce the stress of anticipation, you can help them approach anything in a calmer, more relaxed state. This means they'll be able to make better decisions. It's even useful to not let them out as soon as you get up, or at the same time every morning (excluding puppies or any dogs with toilet training needs). Sometimes I'll let Bodie out when I first get up, sometimes I'll make tea and sit down to work and then let him out a little later. He'll let me know if he really needs to go out, but it means he doesn't get the chance to get used to any specific patterns. There are many benefits for our dogs by ditching the routine. But this is also very useful if you have the chance of a lie-in.

There are a whole series of visual triggers that could be building up your pup's anticipation of going for a walk or just leaving the house (quite possibly one of the highlights of its day). Even if you don't walk at the same time each day, you might not think of all the little signals that you're giving before you even pick up a lead or put on their harness.

What about the more subtle signs - shutting down the laptop, locking the back door, moving towards your keys, changing your shoes. All signals your pup is likely to pick up on and be getting them more and more excited (or worried) about what might be about to happen.

So, what can you do? There are all sorts of things that you can do to stop your pup from picking up on routine signals that lead to them getting over-aroused before you go out for a walk (or you go out to work). Can you change any of the times of day that you go out? I know this can be difficult if you're walking before you head to work or go on the school run, but it's worth thinking about any small ways that you can vary your routine.

In addition to changing the timing of your regular walks, what else can you do differently to ditch the routine?

Here's a list to get you started, but what else can you add?

- Picking up keys and putting them down again without anything else happening. Turn this into a non-event.
- Picking up your pup's harness/lead/collar and not putting them on.
- Picking up the harness/lead/collar and putting them on and taking them off without going anywhere, or just going into the garden.
- Places to walk to – think of going in different directions when you leave the house, how much can you chop and change the walking routes?
- Driving different routes to parks, beaches or woods. Dogs will

recognise the routes you take regularly and their anticipation will start to build.

- Driving somewhere and then staying in the car.
- Searching out different places to go. It's so easy to just head to the places we know but it's good for us as well to experience new things. Some of them are hidden treasures - I've picked up some great recommendations from other dog people in each new space I visit.
- Get them in the car and get them out again without going anywhere (so that even getting in a car isn't so much of an event).
- Types of walks – lead on, lead off, long line on, open spaces, gated dog parks, wooded trails, beaches, canals, pavements, busier areas. What have you got that's around you and how can you use it?
- Vary the length of time that you're out walking or in the park.
- Taking the lead off at different times when you're out (and it's safe and you know your pup's recall is 100% reliable) – not just when you enter the park, you can walk partway before taking it off.
- Putting the lead (or long line) on partway through your walk for a while and then taking it off again. This stops them from thinking that having the lead go on means the end of the 'fun part of the walk.'
- Not going out for a walk at all! Use the time for some training games in the house or garden. You'll be building the relationship you have with your pup. Plus, this can help all sorts of behavioural issues, just contact me if you want any specific recommendations on which games to start with.

Training is something that is happening 24/7, not just when you go to a puppy or dog training class or make a conscious decision to 'do some training.' Any of these little steps above can help your pup be more flexible in their thinking, helping them be calmer in lots of different situations.

Create habits, like calmness, not routines.

PART 2

So far, we've set up the foundations for helping all dogs no matter what their age, breed/type, background, or struggle. **It's a wonderful way of life for all dogs.**

Now I want to work through some examples of how to help dogs in specific areas.

Dogs aren't born with the skills to just walk nicely on a lead by our side. A walk is a human invention. If you observe dogs that are not on a lead, they don't often naturally walk in a straight line, at the same speed for any length of time.

The world we expect our dogs to live in with us has evolved a very long way from the human encampments that dogs first started to scavenge around, tens of thousands of years ago.

Think about how built up and busy our environments are. How much noise, movement, density, and diversity there is in the places we live and visit with our dogs. The volume of people, and other animals. I think it's surprising that more of our dogs don't struggle more in the modern world. It's a testament to how incredibly adaptable they are as a species.

We need to teach them the skills they need for the modern world. And we need to do this BEFORE taking them out for a walk.

In each of the next five chapters, I'll describe how it might look at the moment on your walk. And why your dog might be struggling. Plus I'll talk about the concepts and games that will help.

See which ones resonate most with what you're experiencing at the moment.

7

WALKS AND PUPPIES

What does it look like at the moment?

Puppies aren't born knowing how to trot along happily at our sides. Once the second vaccine dose is effective, the first walks might look like a combination of the following.

- Even if you managed to get the lead and harness on without too much trouble, there is now jumping up and grabbing or biting the lead as you try to walk along.
- At regular intervals their bum is planted firmly on the ground; they're not going anywhere. While you gently tug on the lead trying to get them moving and not understanding why they don't want to go for a walk. It's what dogs are supposed to do!
- They are chasing every exciting new leaf that moves, or blade of grass that waves at them in the wind, pouncing on a fabulous new stick to chomp or finding a stone they can chew on.
- Weeing on, or needing to sniff, absolutely everything – how amazing is the outside world?
- They're running around your legs, perhaps chewing on your

laces or toes. Why did you think flip-flops would be a good idea? You're doing the 'puppy dance' to not get tangled up in their lead, or tread on them. All while not making eye contact with your neighbour who is trying not to laugh at you.

- You stop to talk to someone, and your puppy wants to jump all over them. Or they are barking and lunging on the end of the lead because they're scared of strangers, or they're frustrated that you've stopped.
- Alternating between any or all of the above!

Does any of this sound familiar if you've recently been out walking with a new puppy?

We want to teach our puppies how to walk nicely on a lead at our side. Picture them calmly trotting at a speed that suits us, looking up at us every now and again. There are times when we need to get from one place to another without too much delay and have our dog with us. Dropping the kids off at school for instance.

We want to be able to stop and talk to people without any significant reaction from our puppies. We'd like to be able to go for a walk without stopping to fish foreign objects out of their mouth every few minutes. Oh, and we'd probably like to not have to buy yet another new lead after they're chewed through the last one.

What do we do to change things?

Dogs get better at what they get to practise. So we want to try and limit the activities that mean they do things we don't want them to do.

You start off growing the skills they need in an environment that is the least distracting possible for your puppy. This is probably indoors, in your home. Even the garden will be more distracting than your kitchen or living room. There are so many more exciting things to get distracted by and sniff or chase after, or perhaps get a bit worried about.

We want to make learning anything new, as easy as we can and learning new things often isn't easy. We need to teach them the skills they need for the outside world and grow these skills even BEFORE you start their walks.

How do you get started? Play a couple of games from the list below with a hungry puppy and some of their daily food allowance. It's that simple! Details of the games are all in Chapter 12.

If you read Chapter 3 you know what concepts are. If you didn't, do go back and read this chapter.

Great concepts to grow in puppies:

Calmness
Confidence
Optimism
Focus
Proximity
Novelty

10 great games to start with:

1. Food following
2. Paint the town red
3. Two feet on (front paws)
4. DMT (Distraction Mark Treat)
5. I love my name
6. Toy switch
7. Nose touch (hand targeting)
8. Orientation
9. Middle
10. Boundary games

Keep any games session super short. This might be only three repetitions of a game or 30 seconds. Remember that physically they are still growing and even a sit or a down for a puppy is a workout! Games should be nothing but fun for both of you.

It's better to have a few short games sessions spread out during your day when you can. This also helps them not to get too excited.

Puppies get physically and mentally tired very quickly, even if you think you have a Duracell bunny of a puppy. Although they probably can keep going, they probably can't focus as well and won't learn as much. So it's good to be getting plenty of rest.

Practise the games over a few days or a few weeks. Once they're nailing it in one location, try and play the game somewhere new. If you started in the kitchen on your own with no distractions,

how do they get on in the living room with other people around and/or the TV on? How about in the garden? Don't forget other spaces in your home, like the hallway, the bathroom.

Once you play a game in a new location, with new distractions, it can be like a whole new game for them! Build up their skills with each game before testing it somewhere else.

Can they play the game with someone else?

It's great to get family or friends involved. It creates consistency from other people around your puppy and it teaches them confidence and flexibility to work with people other than just one person. You may need to go back to the early steps of a game when they play it with someone new. Can you share your game-playing skills with other people? Some people will find the mechanics harder than others. But we all get better with a little practice.

Don't be in a rush to take it out of the front door. I know you're desperate to! You can play the game on a lead in the hallway with the front door open or perhaps in the front garden. Break it down into lots of little steps and you'll build up the skills to a great walk much more quickly.

Did you notice that 'Sit' and 'Down' are not on the list of games to start teaching/playing with your puppy? This is often where we want to start, but actually, other life skills are so much more beneficial. Like being **calm** and **confident** and wanting to hang out around you (**proximity**).

Let's talk about socialisation and walks

There is a common misconception that puppies need to play with other puppies for socialisation. It's a term used a lot and I want to touch on what socialisation is, and what it isn't.

What it is…

We want to give our puppies the skills to live calmly, confidently, and happily in the world around them.

Socialisation does include exposure to lots of different experiences and creating positive associations with these experiences. The word positive is important here. This is not about exposing your puppy to the longest list possible. You can do too much, too soon and create a negative experience. Not what we want!

And when we're thinking about the term exposure, this doesn't necessarily mean interaction with something. It can mean being aware of something and learning to ignore it.

There is another part to socialisation.

Socialisation is also about teaching your pup about the concepts of **novelty** and **optimism**. Even with the longest 'socialisation checklist' in the world, it is impossible to introduce our dogs to everything they will ever come across in their lives but we can help them learn that just because they haven't seen, heard, or smelt that new and strange thing before, it doesn't mean that it is bad or scary.

From Chapter 3 on concepts, you might remember that **novelty** is the ability to be confident with things that are new or ambiguous. It's not worrying or exciting to them. **Optimism** is understanding that just because something is unfamiliar, it doesn't mean it's anything to worry about.

Awareness of novelty and pessimism were very effective survival strategies when there were animals around that could kill and eat wild dogs. In most parts of the world, our dogs are very unlikely to get eaten by a wild animal now but the instincts can still be there.

You may have heard about the need for socialisation as early as possible, in the 'critical socialisation period' of three to twelve weeks. Even if you got your puppy at eight weeks old, you are probably past twelve weeks old at the time of reading this.

This puts far too much pressure on new puppy parents feeling the need to expose their young puppy to as many dogs, people, and experiences as possible. All within a few weeks. This can have a negative effect. We want to create positive experiences, so this is not something to rush.

One bad experience far outweighs giving your puppy lots of good experiences. The more we try and cover a long list of things to expose our puppies to, the greater the chance of exposing them to a negative, scary experience. This is a case of quality experiences, not quantity.

How they are responding and feeling to the world around them is so much more important.

It also makes us feel that once we've missed the 'critical socialisation period' then it's too late to do anything about it. What if you got your dog after they were twelve weeks old? I got my rescue pup, Bodie, at eight months old. He'd clearly had little socialisation. Did that mean there was nothing I could do?

Not at all!

By playing games you can help your pup learn that something novel isn't something to be scared of. Or get over-excited by. What we want to work towards is no real reaction at all. We want them thinking "OK I see it, but I'm not bothered about it either way."

What socialisation isn't...

Socialisation isn't letting your dog run around like crazy with any and every dog it meets. Doggy daycare is not socialisation. Busy 'puppy parties' are not socialisation.

Think about what this is teaching them:

- Dogs are mostly more fun than humans. It's really hard for even the most lively of us to compete with four legs (or even three) and a tail!
- It's OK to run off and play with any dog they see.
- Some interactions will be lots of fun.
- Some interactions might not be positive – not all dogs appreciate a lively puppy rushing up to them and can bark, snarl or worse. It is not another dog's job to put a puppy 'in its place.' And it's not good for a puppy to be on the receiving end of this.

It might give you a little relief by wearing them out for a while. But it's quite likely that their arousal bucket will be completely overflowing and make it so hard for them to listen to you for the rest of the walk – or the next time they see a dog. There are plenty of other positive ways to give them the mental and physical enrichment they need.

Control the amount of time your puppy gets to run around and go crazy. Physically they can overdo it very easily, and you could end up with a veterinary bill. Plus they are learning that other dogs are a huge source of fun and excitement; more so than you!

We want our dogs to value their relationship with us over everything else. Don't make this harder for yourself than it needs to be.

They could also get too used to running up to other dogs if you don't have control over them (recall is only recall if it is <u>100% reliable</u>). You don't know how another dog is going to react to your puppy approaching them. You are playing a game of 'Russian roulette' and the possible chance of a negative encounter with a dog that doesn't feel happy about a bouncy puppy running up to them out of control.

Calm introductions to different older dogs can be a great thing. Puppies can learn polite greetings and get used to dogs of different sizes, shapes and colours. These introductions should be with your puppy on a lead so that you have complete control over the introduction. To start with, these introductions might be nothing more than walking towards the adult dog and then turning around and walking away again. What your puppy gets to practise, they will get used to doing. What do you want your adult dog to be doing in a year or two?

Which of your friends (or even friendly people you've seen in the local park) have dogs that would make great doggy roles models?

I didn't start training like this, is it too late?

So, no matter where you are right now, or how old your puppy is, know that you can play games that <u>will help any struggle</u> you are having.

Some clients' dogs are classed as 'senior' dogs (7+ years old) and still learning new things. The earlier you start the better. But it is NEVER too late to teach an 'old dog new tricks.'

8

WALKS AND SCARED OR REACTIVE DOGS

What does it look like at the moment?

Dogs that are scared and/or reactive to things in the environment might look like they are being aggressive but it is much more likely to be the opposite. They are unsure and anxious about something, or downright scared. The trigger might be any dog or certain types or colours of dogs. Or random dogs. Or dogs with testicles! Or people. Or men wearing high visibility clothing. Or children.

Does your dog end up barking and lunging on the end of the lead? Perhaps while you're trying to get your dog out of there as quickly as possible, mumbling apologetically to the person. Or suffer their exclamations about your 'aggressive' dog, when you know you've done everything you could to try and avoid the confrontation from happening.

Or perhaps your dog looks clearly scared - do they crouch down and don't want to go anywhere? Or maybe they are trying to drag you back home or to the car. Or they've dropped flat to the floor and refuse to budge. I know of clients that have had to call their partner to come and collect them because their dog just couldn't move any further.

Do you try to time your walks when as many people as possible are still asleep? Or do you pick routes and locations where you are least likely to see something or someone that could cause a problem? Could a sudden loud noise, like a truck or some thunder, cause your dog to have a meltdown and completely change the outcome of your walk?

This issue may have always been a struggle for them or it might have grown over time. Perhaps it suddenly became an issue after a specific event. Whatever it looks like at the moment, know that it is a very common problem. You are not alone and you CAN change what the current picture looks like for both of you. Give yourself a massive 'well done' for getting this book as part of you looking to do the best for your dog. You are doing an amazing job with them and maybe pour yourself a G&T, a glass of wine or make a cuppa to relax and celebrate while reading this chapter – you deserve it!

What's the full picture? Spot trigger patterns

It is useful to make a note of what it is that triggers any behaviour over a period of time. What patterns are there that you can see? You may notice some trends that you haven't seen before by keeping a diary.

What types of dogs do they react to? Specific colours or sizes? Sex – male or female? Intact – testicles or un-spayed bitches? What about shapes of specific types/breeds - flat faces, pointy ears, curly tails?

The way a dog moves can also be a trigger. It could be a boisterous dog or one that moves quickly. A dog that stands to face another dog straight on with its chest out and tail up is more likely to provoke a response than a dog who is calmly walking or sniffing around.

It can be something specific or something we can't even spot.

What types of people – sex, height, age, clothing types, hair, hats, sunglasses, face masks, uniforms, the pitch of voices?

Places you see the dogs, or people or whatever is causing the reactions? Time of the day? Does it seem to be worse on the second walk in a day?

Does it happen more often the day after they've been to doggy daycare or out with your dog walker? Does it happen more with one person than other people in the household? Does it happen on a certain day of the week (bin/trash/recycling day, weekends)?

Have you noticed any patterns about what they've eaten? Or has there been sickness and/or diarrhoea or more itching than normal?

What else do you notice?

This is not an exhaustive list, but how many of these do you tick off as possible triggers for your dog?

Noises, if so, what kind of noises?

- Loud traffic
- Distant traffic
- Rumbling trucks
- Rattling skateboards
- Horns
- Trains
- Fireworks
- Babies crying
- Children squealing

Unusual things or things in a different context?

- Seeing someone with reflective sunglasses
- A bin bag moving in the wind
- A recycling box
- A man carrying an umbrella
- A woman wearing a facemask
- A horse

Things that move?

- Bikes
- Birds
- Other dogs
- Cats
- Wildlife

It could even be smells that you're unlikely to be aware of.

There are often patterns here – what can you spot? Get observant and use your notes to help you build up a picture.

Why might they have these struggles?

There is a mix of nature (their genetics) and nurture (what happens to them).

A dog's natural temperament and behaviour choices are often passed down genetically (nature). Like a herding breed wanting to herd things, or a sighthound wanting to chase things. But, even then, all dogs are different. Within the same litter, with the same parents and the same start in life, one dog can be very different to another. They all have their own personalities. Some are more confident than others, some are more excitable, and some are naturally calmer.

The environment a dog lives in plays an even bigger role in influencing its behaviour choices (nurture). So what has happened in the past (however long or short), has been a big influence on your dog's personality to date. If you think of your dog's genetics as providing a range of what's possible, a bit like a volume dial. Then the learning experiences dictate where the needle on the dial is set. It could be a series of small events over many years that means your dog has learned to cope with something in a certain way. If every time your dog barked at the window as a worrying looking dog or person went past, the dog or person went away. The barking is learned as a successful behaviour to keep the perceived threat away. Your dog doesn't know that they were never planning to stop!

There is also something called 'flash bulb' learning. If your dog experienced a very stressful event such as being bowled over or even bitten, by another dog the significant event is, in effect, burned into their memory.

The great news is, no matter where your dog is right now, it can change significantly. Whether the issues come from nature or nurture doesn't matter. Whether you know all the history of your dog's life and the reasons behind why they choose to do what they do – it doesn't matter. It can be helpful, but it still doesn't change our approach.

It is also worth knowing that not every reactive dog has had a bad experience.

It is also not your fault.

Whatever the cause of the scared or reactive behaviours, the approach we take is likely to be the same.

What do we do to change things?

We need to help our dogs grow the skills they need before we put them into places and situations where they need those skills. If your dog is reacting negatively on at least half the walks in their week I urge you to stop taking them out on walks for the time being.

I'll repeat that because this is one of the most important points in this book.

If your dog is reacting in any negative way on 50% or more of their walks - STOP taking them out on walks for the time being.

They do not currently have the skills to cope with these walks. They are not enjoyable for them; it is causing them too much regular stress and these walks are likely to be stressful and perhaps upsetting for you.

Every time your dog has a negative reaction to something while out on a walk, they are practising the behaviour that they're doing and they are doing this behaviour because they want to change the way they feel. This might be barking and lunging. This might be pulling you along. It might be dropping flat to the floor and freezing.

The more they do it, the better they get at doing it.

We need to break this cycle! And you can only effectively do this by stopping doing the activity that means it can happen.

Hands up – who is thinking "But won't my dog go crazy at home if I don't take them out for walks every day?"

The short answer is No!

There is so much you can do at home, even in small spaces. You can give them all the mental and physical stimulation they need without ever leaving your front door. You do need to do plenty of other things instead of walks. But it doesn't take longer than the time you are spending on walks. It probably takes less time. I know this might seem like a really scary thing to do but if you seriously want to change things for your dog, you need to do something different. You are not being mean to your dog by not taking them for a walk. You are saving them a lot of stress in their day.

"Insanity is doing the same thing over and over again but expecting different results."

(This quote is often attributed to Albert Einstein but is in fact by Rita Mae Brown).

For most dogs with these struggles, the concepts we want to help grow are:

Confidence
Optimism
Disengagement
Novelty

We can grow these concepts with games, all played at home to start with. You do not need to go for a walk. Sorry, not sorry, I'm repeating myself here, but this does completely go against what we have thought about dogs and what we do with them for so many years.

Eleven great games to get you started (see Chapter 12 for descriptions of the games):

1. Two feet on
2. Noise box
3. Cone game
4. DMT (Distraction Mark Treat)
5. Orientation
6. Middle
7. Bottle knock down
8. Novelty surprise party
9. Boundary games
10. A to B
11. Figure of 8 walking (this is different to a figure of 8 lead)

I couldn't whittle this down to 10 games – you need the extra one!

All of this needs to be happening alongside the three parts of the calmness wheel – **passive calming**, the **calmness protocol** and sufficient **rest**. And you need to 'ditch the bowl'. Still not convinced? You have so much you can do with their daily food allowance!

I didn't start training like this, is it too late?

No matter what age your dog is now, no matter what their background or struggles, know that you absolutely can change what things look like right now. With new knowledge, a little planning and some daily energy and commitment you CAN make significant changes.

Are you ready to get started?

9

WALKS WITH DOGS THAT ARE OVER-EXCITED

(JUMP UP AND DOWN OR PULL LIKE A TRAIN!)

In this chapter, I am going to assume that your dog gets over-excited, and they are not worried or scared by things around them in the environment. If you think any of their behaviours come from being worried make sure you have read Chapter 8 as well.

A dog that is in a state of excitement will struggle to make good choices and they will also find it hard to learn when they are aroused (not in a sexual sense but being excited or stressed).

What does it look like at the moment?

A lot of puppies get very excited by pretty much everything in life! I've covered this in Chapter 7. But teenage and older dogs can also get very excited by the outside world. Some dogs can get more excitable as they get older, perhaps by changes going on around them.

How many of these sentences feel familiar?

- When I'm walking my dog, he just pulls all the time. On the way to the park. Over to each new tree or lamppost or post box.
- She tries to drag me over to see a dog she wants to get to.

- He gets excited just seeing a dog in the same space as us; he 'pogos' up and down, barking or whining with excitement.
- We can be walking along nice and calmly and then he'll suddenly see a cat, or a squirrel and he nearly has me on my face.
- My dog gets so excited when the lead is on, she just keeps jumping up and down at me, biting on the lead. She's chewed through 2 leads already!
- He pulls so much, he's rearing up on his back legs, nearly choking himself.
- To start with the walks are fine, and then once he's played with another dog and he'll run off and won't come back to me. None of the usual food treats or toys makes a difference.
- My dog will jump up at people we don't even know and try to lick their faces.
- My dog humps some dogs (or my leg) at random, it's so embarrassing!
- The day after my dog has been at doggy daycare, she finds it so much harder to listen to me when we're out walking.

Like the dogs that are scared or reactive, it's useful to look at what seem to be the triggers that get your dog too excited. But the reality is, it is likely to be a series of lots of different small events happening, many of which you might not even notice.

Why they might struggle – back to the bucket

In Chapter 3, we covered the arousal bucket that each dog has. If you've got a very excited dog, their bucket is probably quite small, and it only has a small hole at the bottom and there is likely to be lots of small events and/or the odd big event that are all filling up this rather small bucket.

The outcome is that your dog's bucket is regularly or constantly over-flowing - this is when a dog can get very over-excited and make poor choices. Like the examples given in the list above.

Walks, being in parks, off-lead play, open spaces, busy town centres, car rides, seeing other people, dogs or animals can all be bucket fillers for an excitable dog. Some days they may be fine, and then other days it seems like even small things can set them off barking or pulling with excitement.

This is the bucket in action. The more you think about your dog's bucket, the better able you are to control their environment to help prevent the bucket from overflowing in the first place.

For dogs that get over-excited, you don't have to stop walking your dog completely. But you can be more aware of how many times you walk them. Or where you take them. Or what times of the day. Or what you do when you go out.

What do we do to change things?

If they are a teenager, they won't necessarily just grow out of getting too excited. They can have learned a series of behaviours that they like, and they stick with them! Many dogs will naturally become calmer and less excitable as they get older. But you still need to pair growing older with the right games.

There are several areas to tackle with dogs that get really excited.

Limit what is going into the bucket

The more excitable your dog is, the more beneficial it will be to reduce or even cut out walks for a short while. You can replace the walks with games at home that help grow the **calmness** and other concepts you want to work on.

If your dog gets very excited by being in doggy daycare or going on 'pack walks' you might want to consider different options for your dog for a while or think about how you can focus much more on calmness in the days before and after.

When you do go for walks, have a plan of the games you want to play that will help grow the concepts you want more of. See the games list below for some ideas to get you started.

If you have someone in your friends and family circle that likes to take your dog out and chuck a ball around, can you show them some fun games to play instead? Not only is the ball throwing likely to be a big bucket-filler, but it is also probably not doing your dog's joints any good long-term, let alone the risk of a soft tissue injury and an expensive vet bill.

Start the walk off in the right headspace. Think about a little scatter feed or a lick mat before you go out, so they are calmer before you even start.

Grow a bigger bucket and get a bigger hole!

Once you have a bigger bucket and a bigger hole, it doesn't overflow as easily.

For most dogs that struggle with over-excitement, what does the opposite look like?

Number 1 - Calmness

Then the remaining concepts are likely to include:

Disengagement
Focus
Arousal up / arousal down
Thinking in arousal

Ten great games to get you started (see Chapter 12 for descriptions of the games):

1. Two feet on
2. Figure of 8 walking
3. DMT (Distraction Mark Treat)

4. Middle
5. Boundary games
6. A to B
7. Nose touch (hand targeting)
8. Magic hand
9. Disengagement game
10. Eyes on me

Growing **calmness** is the single most effective skill (concept) that will help dogs that get over-excited or struggle to switch off. Every day, be consistent, and you can grow their ability to be calm more of the time.

BITCHES THAT ARE IN SEASON

If you've got a bitch in season, off lead walks are not a very sensible option (unless you don't mind a possible litter of a random cross-breed!). Or you live a really long way from a chance meeting with an uncastrated male dog.

But even on-lead walks are a bit of a risk.

The desire to mate and reproduce is a strong instinctual behaviour (known as a 'drive') and entire males can go to extreme lengths to reach a bitch in season. Her pheromones will be very detectable in the surrounding area. For some of the time, she also will be far more likely to be interested in male dogs. Even well-trained dogs can struggle with recall when it comes to basic sex drive.

Could you physically stop mating from happening between two dogs that were very intent on doing it? Unless your dog is small enough to easily pick up, perhaps not!

She will also attract the interest of other females. And if you are not in a quiet area, your dog may feel anxious with all the additional attention.

Behaviour and hormones

If you've got a female dog, from a behaviour point of view, their hormones can be way more tricky than the boys! Even when there is no risk of unwanted pregnancy, there are still behavioural reasons why you might want to ditch the walks, or at least reduce or change them.

Dogs as a species are unique. After their season, their increased levels of oestrogen, which caused ovulation, fall away. But they have raised levels of progesterone for around 65 days (9 weeks) and this can be a significant influence on how they feel and behave. It's like being pregnant with all of the hormonal behaviours that go with it. Including:

- Increased appetite and/or increased thirst.
- Seeing more value in their resources. Resource guarding issues can get worse.
- Being prepared to compete for something they value. This means an increased risk of an incident over food or toys with other dogs around.
- Loss of appetite, nausea, or morning sickness, much the same as if they were pregnant.
- Lower levels of immunity.
- Being more alert and reactive because they notice more.
- Being more pessimistic.
- Increase or reduction in activity levels. They can go from super energetic to not wanting to do anything.

These are all useful evolutionary symptoms, but not that useful for a calm and happy dog. And this could be going on for two months out of every six months. That's a lot of impact for you and your dog.

All of the above symptoms can add to the bucket filling that is going on!

If you've got more than one bitch that is unspayed, they may well start to sync their cycles and increase the household impact even further so it's easy to see why things can be hard work for you both.

You have alternatives

When bitches are in season and for the following two months, it can help to focus on the following concepts:

Optimism
Calmness

You can add in another concept that's right for your dog at any given time.

It is an individual choice, but I wanted to give you food for thought on not having to take a bitch in season out on a walk. Or in the weeks after their season has finished, you may want to adopt a similar plan to Chapter 8 for Scared or Reactive Dogs. Here are some games that could be an alternative to your usual walks:

1. Two feet on
2. Noise box
3. Cone game
4. DMT (Distraction Mark Treat)
5. FUNder
6. Middle
7. Bottle knock down
8. Novelty surprise party
9. Boundary games
10. Figure of 8 walking

There are plenty of activities you can do in your own home or garden. Pay attention to how your dog is at any given time and be flexible with what you do with them. Being in season means they can go from being lethargic to hyper-active. So try to respond to what your dog needs. You can play more or fewer games depending on what they feel like.

11

PHYSICAL RESTRICTIONS FOR OUR DOGS OR US

This chapter is an interesting one. If I'd been writing this book a couple of years earlier, I probably would have just covered the angle of when our dogs were injured, ageing, or recovering from surgery or we were unable to take our dogs out due to our physical restrictions. But a global pandemic also meant many of us had to look again at how much and where we could take our dogs out.

Let's start with what to do if our dogs might not be able to go on a traditional 'walk'.

Physical restrictions for our dogs

What happens if our dogs need to be on crate rest or limited exercise for a while? Perhaps this is because of an injury or recent surgery. Or perhaps they have health problems that mean they are unable to go for a traditional walk.

Dogs that need to be on crate/pen rest post-surgery and/or lead-only walks, will often still have lots of energy. The calmer you can keep a dog, the quicker they will hopefully heal. But you need to help work their brain (and therefore their nose) to help them cope with being physically less active.

When it comes to crates or pens for recuperation, do follow the advice of your veterinarian. If you are given a choice, my preference is generally for pens rather than crates, or at least bigger crates so that there is space to the side of their bed area. This allows your dog to move around a little more. This means they can choose to get into a position that they find most comfortable. It also means you can add some calming activities that involve some gentle movement like a snuffle mat, puzzle toy or a scatter feed in the area of their pen or crate where their bed isn't.

Physical movement helps move the dog from a state where their sympathetic nervous system is in charge, to a state where their parasympathetic nervous system can kick in. This is important. The sympathetic nervous system is responsible for the production of adrenaline – this is the 'fight or flight' mode. The body can't begin healing in this state of high arousal. The parasympathetic nervous system is the 'resting state' and where healing starts.

Conditions like arthritis and hip or elbow dysplasia, that can make walks painful for our dogs. They don't show pain as we do, and undiagnosed pain is often a factor in behaviour problems. If you are seeing a decline in your dog's behaviour, even just increasing grumpiness in situations that they used to be fine in, or if they seem less interested in their normal walks and activities, do please talk to your vet who may refer you to a Clinical Animal Behaviourist.

And then there is old age, which hopefully our dogs get to experience. In addition to physical decline, there is also mental decline to consider. Canine cognitive decline means structural changes in their brains, which can affect their behaviour. And this very common in older dogs.

The changes can be subtle but are strikingly similar to problems we can have with puppies. They can affect several different areas, including:

- How much time do they spend sleeping?
- Changes to their previous toilet timings and habits. You might need to help them remember where to toilet. And how often they need to go.
- Separation related issues can appear for the first time.
- They might get more frustrated at things, bark at things they didn't used to, or get scared about things they didn't used to (becoming more pessimistic).
- Their hearing and vision are likely to be getting worse.
- And all training areas can go backwards.

The good news is their sense of smell is often the last to deteriorate. So you can make full use of this to provide great enrichment for an ageing dog with poor mobility, poor eyesight, or deafness.

Activities for physical restrictions

There are loads of games to get you started in Chapter 12. With a little imagination, most of these can be adapted to any physical restrictions your dog might have.

Canine enrichment is a great way to look at adding something to our dog's environment that will have a beneficial effect on their lives. Canine enrichment doesn't need to just involve food, there is lots more to it than that.

Passive enrichment - we can add things into their lives that they don't need to interact with. This could include visual enrichment like being able to watch the world go by out of the window. This is assuming this is not a trigger for them getting over-excited or barking! Or how about some auditory enrichment like having the TV or radio on. Music around 60 beats per minute is supposed to be the most relaxing but change it up to keep it interesting.

Active enrichment – there is now a huge range of stuffable food toys like Kongs, lick mats and snuffle mats. You can also include safe things to chew (think about different textures depending on what your dog likes), plus ripping and shredding things up. Cardboard can be great as long as they don't eat/ingest what you give them as long as you don't mind a little mess to clear up afterwards while they're having a snooze.

Scenting games are such a great way to occupy and gently tire our dogs out. How about teaching your dog to play a new scent game? You could go on a **scent walk** – not going very far but stopping and sniffing anything that the dog wants to. You can even encourage sniffing in an area by doing a little **scatter feeding** or sprinkling some dog-safe herbs/spices or playing the **Coin game**. This could be a great transition activity if you just do this out of the front of your house as you reintroduce walks.

How about bringing in scents from a walk that you go on that your dog can't? Rubbing cloths on objects on a walk (trees, lampposts etc.), bag them and bring them back to place around the home to bring the outside scents in. Don't worry about odd looks you might get from strangers!

If your dog doesn't know the names of specific toys, you can teach them the name of a toy and ask them to go and find it.

Digging is a very natural behaviour for our dogs. Could you include a digging area in the garden? If you put it on a cue, you may save other areas of your garden. Perhaps a sandpit with a lid to avoid any unwanted 'sandy candy' from local cats.

ACE (Animal Centred Education) Free Work was developed by Sarah Fisher to observe how our dogs move. But it is also a great way for dogs to grow **confidence** and use their nose, mind and body to explore the world around them. Include a couple of water bowls, one raised a little, one on the floor.

You just need a little space and some household objects. Look for different textures and heights that your dog can walk on, step on to, move around, put their nose or head in. Use a variety of different foods – textures and flavours to encourage your dog to explore. How they explore is completely up to them; there is no right or wrong way. Feel free to give a little gentle encouragement. You can search for 'free work dogs' on YouTube to find out more.

Restrictions on our movement

But what if we have a short-term injury or are recovering from surgery? Or perhaps there is a life-long condition that means traditional walks out with our dog are not always possible or easy or mentally we feel unable to go outside.

Or what if there was a global pandemic that meant certain areas in the world were in complete lockdown for some time? Oh hang on...

Early 2020 threw a massive curveball at the world that impacted everyone differently and put restrictions on many of us, as to when and where we could go out walking our dogs. Perhaps you were only allowed to take your dog out for toileting or a short walk once a day. A few years ago, this might have been unimaginable, but 2020 changed that.

At the start of the first lockdown in the UK, I also fractured my foot. I was in plaster up to my knee for eight weeks, so I had a small taste of not being able to walk our energetic young Bodie. I was fortunate to have my partner Ash to take him out when we were allowed to but it taught me to be resourceful and work out ways to adapt games to play them in our home or seated on a chair in the garden.

The flexibility of being able to effectively exercise your dog physically and mentally when we're not able to go out for a 'walk' is invaluable. Now, for more reasons than ever.

I still use the training videos I created in our garden with me stiffly walking about in a cast or playing seated games!

Training games can be adapted to play seated if you are unable to move around freely. All you need is a little imagination. Even playing games like **FUNder** and **Leg weaves** can be adapted to go under or around your chair. See Chapter 12 for all of the games.

Do you have days when you don't feel physically or mentally able to go into the outside world? Please don't feel guilty about not being able to take your dog for their usual walk. If you are up to it, play some games around the home or go to the list of **Passive calming** activities for great brain-tiring activities for them.

Even simple toy and/or food-finding games around the home can be a fun game for your pup. Using their nose is a lovely way to tire them out in a small space. You hide the treasure while they wait (in another room or someone holding them). Then release them to 'find it'. Help them if they need it and have big celebrations when they find it.

And, of course, ask for help when you need it. A local support system is important for all of us, but even more so if you are looking after a dog single-handedly.

12

LET THE GAMES BEGIN

In the words of Absolute Dogs – there's a game for that!

Being able to reshape our dogs' brains through games is one of the joys of owning a dog! Why wouldn't we want to play games with them every day?

I want to help guardians and dog-lovers to think differently.

If we have a dog, it's easy to think:

> *"Of course I need to walk my dog every day."*

Or

> *"A tired, exhausted dog is a good thing."*

I want to change that to:

> *"Of course I play games with my dog every day."*

Or

"My dog gets mental and physical stimulation every day."

(And this may or may not involve leaving the home).

In this chapter, I walk you through how to play the games listed in previous chapters. However, it is easier to demonstrate the games on video. You can watch videos of these games by registering for your bonus videos here https://go.puptalk.co.uk/book-games/

The games covered in this chapter are just a taster of the games that exist. There are well over 200 games already, and they're growing all the time. The more targeted you can get with playing the games to help your dog's specific struggles the better. If you want help identifying which games are the ones you need right now, reach out to me.

The games in this chapter are great starters for most dogs. The names of most of the games in this book are courtesy of Absolute Dogs

With all of the games, less is definitely more. With young puppies, a game may have 3 repetitions and only take 30 seconds. With an older dog, this might be 5-10 repetitions and take 1-3 minutes. It is more fun for both of you, and therefore much more likely to be effective, if you only play games in short bursts.

I've listed the games in alphabetical order to make it easier for you to refer back to and find them. They are not in the order in which you need to play them What you and your dog play can be completely tailored to you.

Games can be physically and mentally tiring. You may be surprised how 10 minutes of games can settle your dog down. More so than a 30-minute walk.

There are lots more tips on how to get the best out of the games and every aspect of your dog training in Chapter 15.

Some useful foundation terms

In some of the games, you will read the terms **attraction noise**, **luring**, **release cue** and **shaping**. We use these in lots of different games. So let's go through what these mean now.

Attraction noise

We tend to overuse our dogs' names; it can become 'white noise' and if we sometimes use it when we're not happy with them, this gives them even more reason to tune out to it but there are lots of times when we want to get their attention – a look towards us or they start to come back us. There is no need to call their name. Experiment with a little **attraction noise** like a 'kiss kiss' or horsey 'click, click' sound. It can help them connect back with you, especially if they've wandered off and got distracted.

Luring

The term **luring** just describes how we use food right in front of our dog's nose to encourage them to do the behaviour that we want them to do, to get them to move through space by following the food in your hand.

How we do this is by holding something tasty that our dog likes to eat and having our hand very close to their nose and mouth. If we move our hand very slowly, our dog is fairly likely to try and follow to get the food.

The trick with luring is to go <u>very</u> slowly so we can feel the wetness of their nose. If you lose connection with their nose, they generally stop following and may give you a **sit** or lay **down** as they try to work out what it is they need to do to get the food.

Don't go too long before releasing the food (it may only be a couple of seconds). We don't want them to get nippy trying to get the food or get frustrated and give up and wander off.

If luring isn't working, try moving your hand even slower! They should be licking and nibbling as you move your hand. Or use food that they find irresistible.

Release cue

A **release** cue is like a reset button or a pressure release for our dogs. Some people use the word command instead of cue, but to me, this implies it's an order Movement changes how they feel, so getting them moving can help prevent them from getting 'stuck' and unable to work out what it is you want them to do. It can also help them to get 'unstuck' if they're just standing or sitting in front of you looking confused.

What word do you use? You can use any word that makes sense to you. Some people use 'break!' or 'free!' or 'OK!'. Pick one word to start with and be consistent. (You can use more than one word once your dog is used to release cues).

How do you do it? Give the cue 'break/OK/free' and throw a piece of food a moment afterwards. It's always the word first followed by the food. With practice, we are looking for the dog to move, or at least twitch, when we give the cue. The food is giving the initial reason to move and the reinforcement for following the release cue.

It's a good idea to use your release cue after say 2-5 repetitions of pretty much any training game you're playing. We want our dogs to love their release cue as much as they love the game they're playing! You can build up the desire for both over time.

Shaping

Shaping is breaking down a behaviour into small steps, that build-up towards the end behaviour that you want. You are practising and rewarding each small step. Shaping can be so useful for dogs that get easily frustrated and need to be rewarded for smaller steps before they give up on something new that they don't understand.

If you were shaping a rollover, for instance, you might start with luring and rewarding them when they are in a **down**. Then you might lure and reward for a **look back** over their shoulder. And then **lifting a front paw** as they look back. Building the small steps until they were able to **roll over** in one movement.

Mark and reward

Throughout the games, you will see various instructions to '**mark**' and '**reward**'. Here's a quick guide if this is new to you. Plus a few tips on how to do it effectively to get the most out of your dog training.

To mark something means to give a short audible or visual cue that tells your dog, at the moment, that they did what you wanted them to.

I like to use something super simple like 'yes!' It's short and I make it sound bright. You only need to say it once.

Some people like to use a clicker. This is also a really precise way to mark the exact point that your dog did something right. I don't tend to use one because I like to keep my hands free to handle food, toys, their lead or anything else I need. But it's a personal choice; some people love them.

Visual markers also work well – and are essential for deaf dogs. For instance, a thumbs up cue to replace the 'yes!' or the click.

The reward is something that closely follows after the marker, to reinforce what your dog did with something that they enjoy. It could be food, toys, praise, or physical contact.

Make sure the reward is really rewarding. We want to cement the learning where your dog did what you wanted them to. Tasty food is often the quickest and easiest form of reward for training games.

Try experimenting with different 'values' of food. When you are working on a new game or a game that they find harder, try the foods that your dog loves. When I started playing boundary games with Bodie he was not enjoying it enough if I played it with his dry food. If I had some cheese, chicken, or hotdog, he would be a lot more interested!

Toys can also be a reward. For instance, you can introduce the toy to play with after a few repetitions of a game you're growing. But it is harder to get repetitions of a game. This is more for experienced dogs.

A calm stroke can be a reward for some dogs. And it can work well in some circumstances.

If you can be precise about how you mark and reward, your dog will find it easier to know and understand what it is that you wanted them to do. This makes it easier for them to do it again. And get better at it.

Marker and reward tips:

- Don't keep repeating your marker. Once is enough, just make it precise as to when you use it.
- Try to avoid giving the food reward and then following it up with a fuss, unless your dog genuinely finds this rewarding. I see quite a few dogs shy away from this.
- I recommend not using your dog's name as a marker. If we use their name less frequently, it has more effect. Get used to not saying it if you can and remember your **attraction noise**.

And now for the games…

The games are in alphabetical order. You only need to play the games that are right for you and your dog. Play them in any order that works for you.

Two feet on (front paws)

Concepts
Body awareness, confidence, disengagement, engagement, fitness, focus, optimism, proximity.

What it does

Two feet on is a great game to boost confidence and optimism. It's also good for creating body awareness.

Dogs often aren't very aware of where their legs and feet are!

I love to play this one when I'm out and about. It can be great to make a walk more interesting – look out for low walls or natural obstacles like logs, tree stumps and large stones to play it anywhere. It can get your dog engaged with you but in a calm way; no ball chasing is needed. It's a really useful way to see if they can still listen and focus in the middle of doing something more exciting.

It can help a dog to stay engaged and connected with you. This can help dogs that get over-excited by the environment (yes this is Bodie). But it also helps dogs that get worried by the environment and are constantly scanning for the next potentially worrying dog/person/delivery van. It gives them something productive to focus on and do with you.

It can also be really helpful for dogs who jump up at people. **Two feet on** 'grounds' them somewhere appropriate so they can be 'up' saying "hi" but their paws are somewhere that is not on the clean clothes of guests!

How to play it

Pick an object that is low to start with. You want something quite solid, not slippery, and not taller than the height of their front legs (and probably lower to start off with, especially if your dog is nervous or your puppy is young, and they are still growing).

It could be a book that is only 4-5cm tall. Or a low plastic step, or a yoga block. Be resourceful and have a look around your home for something suitable.

We are going to lure our dog towards the object and just feed them for being near it to start with, especially if they are nervous.

Once they're confident enough, lure them towards and up and on to the object. Mark ('yes!') and reward (with daily food or higher value treats) for any move towards the object. It might be just a raised paw, or it might be one paw on it. Reward for all their attempts to start off with.

Once they are putting 1 or 2 paws onto your object, feed 2 or 3 pieces of food in this 'end position'. We want to clearly reinforce that this is what we want them to do.
Only when they are reliably stepping up onto the object should you add in the cue. I tend to use 'front paws' but you can say whatever you like.

If there is any chance of the object moving, hold on to it with your hand or foot to make sure it doesn't slip and cause a scare.

After 2 or 3 goes at this, add the release cue. Say your cue 'Break!' and follow with throwing a piece of food a short distance to get them moving away from you and the object.

You only need to play this for a minute or less (especially for a puppy). Keep it short and play it again another day.

Bodie is quite a big dog and will now happily give **Two feet on** a recycling box or park bench at nearly every opportunity. The end position of standing with his front paws on an object is rewarding in itself for him now.

Troubleshooting and variations

To start with your dog may not be comfortable stepping on to something new. You might even need to just feed them calmly around this object that isn't normally in this position until they are more confident.

If your pup is struggling to take a step forward, once you add in the release cue, when they come back towards you, they might offer you a better attempt than they did the time before.

You can also place the object between you and your pup. As they gravitate back towards you for the next piece of food, they may naturally step onto the object.

If your pup is jumping up onto the object, with all 4 (or 3) paws, slow down the luring and hold the food in position so that they stop once their front paws step up.

Over time, you'll get better at knowing where to lure them to help them understand what it is you want them to do.

When you're out on walks and in parks, look out for any object that's a good height to play this game.

You can play it using your knee if you can crouch down on a walk. Or on your lap, if you're seated somewhere.
For any game that's not working, give it a break and have another go another time.

———

A to B

Concepts
Disengagement, focus, resilience.

What it does
This is one of the best 'management' games for using on walks. But it needs to be practised before using it on a walk.

Sometimes you can find yourself heading towards something you'd rather not have to face. If you have a dog that reacts to dogs, you probably try to walk them somewhere where you're not likely to see another dog. And then one just appears around a corner when you weren't expecting it. Your dog might now be barking and lunging on the end of the lead.

Don't feel bad; these things happen. This game gives you a great tool to help handle future situations. So get practising it now!

A to B is a brilliant game to help manage a situation when other games won't work. This is your 'let's get out of here' game! This might be your dog staring at another dog (or person) coming towards you and they are too worried or too excited to look away. It might be that they are pulling you over to something. Or they're stuck and can't move forwards.

What you're saying with your actions is "You're coming with me, it's non-negotiable and it's a great deal for you!" This is not about you dragging your dog away.

This is a game you play at home or in a quiet space so that it becomes a practised game for both of you. It becomes a physical autopilot manoeuvre.

Then in the face of something challenging, the training kicks in, your mechanics are smooth, and it just works! You will feel calmer when you are out walking, knowing that you have an effective strategy for things you can't predict.

How to play it
This game works best with a harness with a front and back clip or a single point harness and a collar (or headcollar if you use one). The key is using a double-ended lead or two leads if you feel resourceful. This gives you two physical points of contact between you and your dog.

Step 1
Get your dog used to the feeling of you sliding your hand down the two leads towards your dog. You want to make sure they are comfortable with your hand being near them in this situation. The hand that is on the same side as your dog is the one that slides down the lead.

You can hold the top of the lead with the other hand. When your sliding hand is close to your dog, feed your dog from that hand.

Let's say your dog is on your right, slide the right hand down the leads, pulling the 2 parts of the lead closer together. When your right hand is close to your dog, feed with the right hand. Your dog will feel the difference through the two points of contact because your hand position changed. You are just teaching them that this sensation is a good thing! Practise it a few times in the home or garden.

Step 2
Now we want to add in 180-degree movement with a brisk cue.

If our dog is on our right, slide your right hand down the leads, turn your body in the opposite direction with a bright 'Let's go!' and feed as you go (if they can take food at this point). You can have a piece of food in your right hand as it slides down the lead ready to feed as you walk away.

Be confident with the turn, head up and be bright with the cue. With practice, your dog should follow with you quite readily. If you are playing this game in your garden with something tasty in your hand and no big distractions around you, you are setting your dog up to get it right.

With repetition, the sensation of your hand sliding down the leads is the signal to them that you're on the move in a different direction.

You can practise this game with you going around the outside or the inside of your dog. If the distraction is significant, it can be easiest to make sure you are on the outside of your dog so that you are a physical barrier between them and the distraction.

You can also practise on both sides. Most of us find one side easier than the other. But it's great for flexibility for both of you to be able to start this one from either side.

Troubleshooting and variations
The mechanics of holding the lead, and delivering food take a little practice. Be kind to yourself if it doesn't feel right. You are also working with a dog that doesn't yet know what you want them to do.

Practise it somewhere quiet, before you need it. This is not about yanking your dog away from something. This is a smooth, practised movement, that is really effective at that moment.

If your dog is faced with something scary or very exciting, they may not be at all interested in the food as you A to B. But it can help build up the practise sessions nicely. If you put the practice in, it can become an automatic reaction for your dog without food being needed.

———

Bottle knock down

Concepts
Confidence, flexibility, grit, novelty, optimism.

What it does
I love this game! This is a great game for confidence building and this is worth topping up for all of our dogs. It also helps grow their optimism around noises, movement, and novel objects.

It also helps our dogs get used to noises. For dogs that bark at, or are scared of noises, it can help them get more used to sounds that they make themselves.

This is also a great brain game, great for low impact fun and small spaces. It's one you can play anywhere.

How to play it

All you need is a plastic bottle or container with a screw lid or top. Pick a size that's not too big for your dog. For puppies and smaller dogs pick something like a 500ml size. For bigger dogs, you could use a 1-1.5 litre bottle.

Add a small amount of water to the bottle and put the lid on. A couple of finger widths of water will be fine. You just want to add a little weight to help it stand up, but not make it too heavy.

Step 1

To start with pop the bottle down in front of your pup and 'mark' and reward them (give them a piece of food) for looking at it or stepping towards it. Be accurate with when you say your marker and say it only once.

You can do this a couple of times. Add in your release cue like 'break' and throw a piece of food away. When they come back towards you, mark any look or step towards the bottle again.

Step 2

Now we'd like our dogs to touch it, with a nose or a paw.

If at any stage they ignore it, pick it up and hold it behind your back for a moment. And then put it down on the floor again. Because it disappeared, they can become more interested in it allowing you to mark and reward something that is closer to what you want.

Or you can give your release cue and throw a piece of food away. Getting them moving helps to get their brain moving too, so when they trot back over to you, they can often try something else that might be what you wanted.

If they happen to knock it over (on purpose or by accident), it's big rewards (several pieces of food) so they know they did a great job!

If they get distracted and start to wander off, you can make your **attraction noise** to see if they want to come back and carry on. If you've played a few repetitions, perhaps that's enough for today. Come back to it another day.

Troubleshooting and variations

If your pup is particularly nervous, I'd start by just placing some pieces of food on the floor somewhere near the bottle so that they get comfortable with this new strange object. Once their confidence grows, then you can move to step 1 above.

If your pup doesn't know what you want, they will often try something they do know to try and get the reward. This might be a 'sit' or a 'down'. Don't reward this here, it will confuse them on the rules for this game. Just give the release cue and see if they try something else when they come back to you.

If they are struggling to engage with the bottle (but NOT if they're scared) try popping a piece of their food on top of the bottle lid for them to get. You can then mark this close interaction with the bottle. They may even knock it over by accident – another opportunity to give a big reward).

You can add more water to make the bottle harder to knock over. Or you can replace the water with kibble/dry food to make it noisier.

Think about the surface you play it on. Carpets and rugs will make less noise. Hard floors will be much louder.

Start quieter and only make it noisier when you are sure they are confident enough. You don't want the bottle to scare your pup.

You can also play it with different sizes and shapes of containers to help your dog's confidence with novel objects.

I like to combine this game with Boundary games that you'll read next. Come off the boundary to knock the bottle over, and then hop back up onto the boundary.

———

Boundary game

Concepts
Arousal up/arousal down, calmness, disengagement, drive, focus, impulse control, independence, resilience, self-control.

What it does
Boundary game is one of the most versatile games you can ever play. There are so many levels and variations to it – I could write a whole book on boundary games! So here, I will just give you the general principles to get you started.

This super-simple game teaches your pup to happily go to a specific bed or place. And stay there and chill out, until you say it's time to come off the boundary and do something with you.

You can use it to grow calm at home at any time. You can have a dog that can be calm with visitors coming around or deliveries at the door. Or you can help them switch off in the park or a café. Or you can help them to grow their sense of independence – great if you've got a dog that follows you around the house, even into the bathroom!

How to play it

Use your dog's daily food allowance (high or low value as you need). You can get through quite a lot of food with this game – but you have ditched the bowl, right?

Pick a 'boundary'. This can be anything you like - a bed that they already use, their crate, a towel, a jumper, or a chair. The principals are all the same. To start with, it can help to have something with sides so that there is a definite place of being on or off the boundary.

These are the first 6 steps to get you started:

Step 1

You are giving a reward for any interaction they make with the boundary. This can just be looking at it, stepping towards it or putting a paw on it.

What you are doing is showing them where the value is. Place the food on the boundary rather than giving the food straight to them. We want them to see the value as coming from the boundary, rather than directly from your hands.

You can have the boundary immediately in front of you so that they naturally gravitate towards you and onto the boundary. Until they understand the game, the visual cue of where you stand can help.

There are no cues that you are giving them at this stage (you're not telling them to go to their bed, or sit etc. Just let them choose to interact with the boundary and calmly feed the boundary when they do. Absolutely no nagging to get them to come back to you or the boundary. You can throw a piece of food on the bed so that they naturally orient to you (and the bed) for more food.

Step 2
Reward their choice to get completely onto the boundary, with NO verbal cue. You want them to love the boundary! To choose the boundary. This game is so powerful because they will be making good choices for themselves. Feed them for getting on the boundary.

Step 3
Feed them lots - be generous when they're on the boundary. We want to build up them choosing to stay on the boundary, so drip-feed some food (again onto the bed, not directly to your dog). Calmly deliver the food, slowly feed the bed and then even slower!

There are no cues to go into a 'sit' or a 'down.' No cues to 'stay.' Let your dog choose to help them grow calmness in the long run. If they do come off the boundary, it's not a problem, they just don't get a piece of food at that point.

Step 4
Now we are going to add in a release cue. I like to use 'break'. Throw a piece of food a moment after giving the cue. Timing is important - you want your dog to love the release cue as much as jumping back onto their boundary. This teaches them to stay on the boundary until you say it's time to come off it.

Step 5
Wait for your dog to choose to get back on the boundary. This doesn't need a cue yet. Make sure there are big rewards when they first choose to get back on the boundary. You are building up your dog's love of being on the bed AND waiting for the release cue.

Step 6
Always end a boundary games session with a release cue. In time, we want them to understand that when they get onto their boundary, they

stay there and chill out until we say it's time to get off and come and do something else.

Step 7 and beyond

Over time we are looking to build calmness when your dog is on the boundary. We do this by rewarding changes in their position, getting progressively more relaxed. This is going from a 'stand' to a 'sit' to a 'down' (this is their choice, not a cued behaviour).

Remember you are just calmly drip-feeding the boundary. If you have a very busy dog, you just have to capture the moments of relative calmness!

If they get on the boundary when you're not specifically training - you don't need to give a release cue. It's just become a place they like to hang out (or it's their bed/crate where they like to rest already).

There are many more levels to add to this game, but that will get you started if you've not played the boundary game before.

Troubleshooting and variations

Play about with where your body is to start with. Your pup may find it easier if you are sat on the floor by the boundary. Or standing next to it. Try different positions to see what helps them work out the 'rules' of the game.

You can also drop the odd piece of food down onto the boundary to encourage them to come back to it. There is no need to call their name, although a little attraction noise like a 'kiss kiss' sound can help them come back to the game if they've wandered off and got distracted.

Like all games, keep these games short (a few minutes) to start with. This can build up to a much longer game with an experienced dog that loves its boundary.

If your dog is not that into boundary games, use higher value food to help with motivation to start with.

———

Cone game

Concepts
Confidence, engagement, flexibility, focus, optimism, resilience, thinking in arousal.

What it does
This is a great game to boost confidence. You are teaching them to pop their head in a cone (or a yoghurt pot, beaker etc.) and they are covering their nose, perhaps their eyes and it's touching their ears. This grows their confidence and sense of optimism.

In an ideal world, all dogs should be muzzle trained. If your dog is ever injured or needs to have treatment that could be painful, the vet will probably need to put a muzzle on them. If you have got your dog comfortable with a muzzle already, this is one less thing to add to their stress in the situation.

This game is also a great foundation to introduce dogs positively to new pieces of equipment like head collars, harnesses, coats, and fleeces. See Chapter 16 for 'changing the picture' of walks for our dogs.
It's also just a great game to play in a small space to have fun.

How to play it
When I say cone, I mean any object that your dog's nose/muzzle will fit into. It could be a yoghurt pot, beaker, whatever you have to hand.

Introduce the 'cone' to your dog. We just want to make sure that they are not worried about it to start with.

If your dog is trying to bite it or run off with it, don't let them. We don't want them to practise what we don't want them to do, even if it does make you laugh!

Step 1
Reward them for any interaction with the cone – a look, a step towards it, perhaps a sniff. Mark them precisely with a 'yes' (or your marker word) and give them a piece of food. We are 'shaping' any interaction with the cone.

It can help to hide the cone behind your back. When you bring it out in front of you, it can be more interesting because it's suddenly appeared. Therefore your dog is more likely to be interested in investigating it.

If they're not interested in it, pop it behind your back for a moment and then try again.

Step 2
Hide the cone behind your back again before popping it out in front of you. Keep the cone at nose height to your dog. You are looking for your dog to do a little more over time. From looking at it to sniffing it, to popping their nose in it. Don't forget your marker – every time they do the behaviour that you want. And follow up straight away with their reward.

In between a few repetitions, add in a release cue. Throw a piece of food away from you, let them eat it and then they may offer you something else when they come back towards you. You can hide the cone behind your back at any point, and bring it out again to create more interest.

You can also try popping a piece of food just inside the mouth of the cone so that they can eat it easily (as long as they're not scared of the cone).

Step 3

As your dog gets better at this game you can wait for a little more before giving the mark and reward. This could be putting their nose right into the cone.

Or it could be bobbing their head into the cone 2-3 times before giving the mark and reward.

Keep using the release cues to keep them moving. If ever they get 'stuck' and don't seem to know what to do, the release cue gets them moving physically and helps their brain to work too.

Troubleshooting and variations

You can start with **Nose touch** to get your dog used to come in towards your hands. This is especially useful with nervous dogs.

Don't try and push too hard with this game if your dog is nervous about the cone. Look at their body language. Is their weight on their back legs? Are they reluctant about coming forwards? Your pup might be a little nervous or unsure about this new situation (even if they don't look it). If they are holding back, make it easier for them by just letting them have some food from the floor or your hand with the cone somewhere at a distance that they are comfortable with.

If your dog is trying to bite the cone, you can try putting it under your arm to avoid the edges being so easy to grab or play it when they are a little calmer.

Play it with different objects to get your dog confidently stuffing its head into all sorts of containers!

You can play this game with new pieces of equipment like head collars, harnesses etc. Try to create a big loop from part of the item to feed your dog through initially.

Then work on them putting their nose/head through the item instead of the cone. If you alternate the object they already know with a new item it can help them understand what game they are playing.

You can play variations of this game with a veterinary medical collar, Elizabethan collar or 'cone of shame.'

How cool would it be if your dog wags their tail when you get out a medical collar?

If you want to get prepared, get your dog a muzzle to play the game with. Research what type of muzzle is best for your breed of dog. Do make sure it is one of the designs where they can pant, breathe freely, drink and eat. A basket muzzle will do this. Take measurements and make sure it is the right size and a comfortable fit.

Follow all the steps above inter-changing the cone and the muzzle in the middle of the game.

A word about muzzles

There are still stigmas around muzzles. Muzzles are a great tool when used in the right way.

- If you have a dog that is prone to picking up and eating rubbish or poop, muzzles can help.
- It doesn't necessarily mean a dog is dangerous.
- It could be that they get anxious when other dogs approach them and perhaps this could cause them to snap or bite.
- It could be that the dog has a high prey drive and could potentially chase and catch something small and furry.
- Take the stress away from your dog during a vet visit; make sure they are already comfortable with wearing a muzzle.

Whatever the reason, muzzles are a sign of a responsible and thoughtful dog guardian.

If you see someone with a dog with a muzzle on, can you smile (and say hello if you're close enough). It's easy for people to feel judged and a bit isolated. They may be working hard on some behavioural issues and a smile from you could go a long way!

You could incorporate this game with **Boundary games** by calling them off the boundary for a minute of Cone game and then back to the boundary.

————

DMT (Distraction Mark Treat)

Concepts
Arousal down, calmness, confidence, disengagement, focus, optimism, proximity, resilience.

What it does
There are distractions all around our dogs so much of the time. This game teaches our dogs not to worry or get over-excited about any of it. You are effectively saying to them "Yes I see it too, but it's nothing to do with us."

Everyone needs DMT in their bank of go-to games!

How to play it
When you see a distraction (D), mark (M) it with a word and deliver the treat (T).

Start off practising this game when there isn't a distraction. You need to get used to playing the game, and your pup needs to learn the marker word means a tasty reward.

"What word shall I use?" You can use any word that feels right to you. A lot of us Absolute Dogs folks like 'Niiiice'. Some people I know use 'Caalm' or 'Eeeasy'. It doesn't matter. Just make the word sound relaxed and mellow. Extend the sound – ham it up a bit!

It is important to build this one up with little or no distractions around. We want to build a reflex action of looking around for food when you say the marker word.

The more you build, the greater the level of distraction that it will work for.

Without putting the practice into DMT, when your pup has seen something they find distracting, they are probably not able to listen or be interested in the treat.

The treat can be a toy as well as a food reward. But this can be hard to deliver calmly. And you only have one opportunity to reward rather than having multiple pieces of food.

Troubleshooting and variations

The more intense the distraction, the higher value the reward will need to be. If you are using dry food/kibble and you're trying to combat an exciting squirrel, it's going to be hard. If you have got a smelly piece of hot dog available, you might at least make their nose twitch in your direction.

You can't play this game too much. For the first year of Bodie being with us (he was a very excitable teenager with no training), we would use half of his daily food playing DMT on any of his walks. In hindsight, we should have been walking him less and playing games in the garden more, but I hadn't researched and written this book when we first rehomed him!

If your dog is unable to take the food after you've said the marker word, the distraction is too exciting, too close, or too worrying and you need to build up the power of the game in easier situations and at a greater distance.

————

Figure of 8 walking

Concepts
Arousal up/arousal down, calmness, disengagement, fitness, focus, novelty, proximity.

What it does
This is our go-to game for our walks with Bodie. It can help to lower arousal levels (excitement), and we use it at various times at the start, middle and end of a trip to a park or a road walk.

It can help with disengagement from the environment – anything that your dog finds exciting or worrying. Once you have practised playing this game, your dog is more readily able to walk in the Figure of 8 pattern with you and focus on you.

It's really useful for a physical warm-up. Injuries can happen more easily if you've just arrived at the park and your dog starts tearing around with another dog.

It's also great for fitness. Walking at a slow pace means your dog has to use their core muscles more than if they were trotting at their natural speed. They are using all 4 (or 3) legs independently. It's surprisingly hard work for them.

Please note: Figure of 8 walking is a training game to play with your dog. A figure of 8 slip lead is a piece of equipment and not what I'm describing here.

How to play it
Like all new games, this is so much easier to start somewhere with the
least distractions. If not a garden (or big enough space indoors), find a
quiet space or car park. Hard surfaces are normally easier than grass;
there are less interesting smells to get distracted by.

This game is so much easier if you use the following equipment:

- A double-ended lead (or 2 leads).
- With a harness with front and back clips.
- Or a collar or head collar and harness.

Have each of your hands separately on the lead (or leads), imagine you
are holding the reins of a horse. This gives 2 points of connection
between you and your dog.

Pick two points on the ground to walk around - trees, bollards, lampposts,
plant pots in the garden - whatever you have. With Figure of 8 walking,
we're looking for a flowing, fluid movement that promotes a calm
emotional state. By going over the same area several times the amount of

sniffing should reduce.

It can look staggered and stiff to start with! It's not always as easy as it looks. There is no dragging or jerking your dog. You have your head up and you are walking with purpose.

You're looking for moments where they match you. If they're jumping up and bouncing, try slowing it down.

You are just walking. Look where you're going, not down at them.

You don't have to use food for this game. Adding food can make it more exciting and we are looking for calmness. If you need some food to get them moving with you, try it and see how it works for you.

Don't let them walk across you if you can help it. Keep them on one side of you. But it is good to practise with them walking on both sides. Sometimes you can be on a pavement or path where you want to have them on a specific side for traffic or another dog for instance. It's good for both of you to be flexible.

If it doesn't work for you at first, please keep trying.

Little by little your dog will get better at connecting and mirroring you. This one can test your patience, but it is worth sticking at it.

Troubleshooting and variations
Try not to look down at your dog to see what they are doing. With your head up facing the direction you are walking; they are more likely to go with you.

It doesn't have to be in the specific pattern of a figure of 8. It could be zig zags to help break your dog's eye contact if they are staring at dogs as they approach. It could be in a circle or oval shape.

Keep your dog on the opposite side to where a distraction is. This will help them.

If they get stuck and won't move, you can use the game A to B to get them moving again. Perhaps 'We're walking' rather than 'Let's go!'.

———

Food following

Concepts
Confidence, engagement, focus, grit, optimism, proximity, resilience.

What it does
This is a fabulous foundation game for puppies, any dog that is new to playing games with food or a dog that isn't that keen on going near your hands.

This game is great for growing optimism – once they understand the game, it is easy for them to 'win' some food before tackling something a little harder. You can use it as a good 'warm up' game.

We want to help build up their association of our hands being a source of great things, i.e. food! And not just seeing our hands as things that stop them from doing something they want to do (like stopping the fun by putting on the lead or putting them in a pen or crate).

It is also a starter game to help dogs get used to following food generally. This is a useful skill when we start throwing the food around!

How to play it
Have one piece of food in your palm, held in place with your thumb.

With the food in your hand, have your hand at nose height to your pup with your palm facing their nose.

Start quite close so that they know you have the food and start gently moving your hand away from them. As soon as they start to follow, release the piece of food.

Start with really slow movements and let them get their nose right on the piece of food. You can even let them lick or gently nibble on the piece of food. We tend to move too far or too quickly, and they don't yet know the game is to follow your hand to get the piece of food. If you have already taught **Sit** or **Down**, they may well try that to see if that's what you want them to do!

Reload with another piece of food and repeat a few times.

As they get better at following the food you can increase the speed and distance that you're moving your hand.

From a few inches to a few feet. Try to keep your palm facing their nose, you can flick your wrist around making a figure of 8 shape parallel to the floor.

You can also switch from one hand to the other, doing a kind of food relay!

Troubleshooting and variations
If your dog is getting over-excited by the food, play it with the lowest value food you have (kibble rather than treats, or veggies rather than kibble?). Play it for a very short time (30 seconds) and/or play it when they are calmer.

If your dog isn't that into their food, play this game when they are hungry. And with something that they find super tasty. Let them have the food

LET THE GAMES BEGIN

quickly from under your thumb so that they 'win' easily and want to try again.

If holding the food in your palm with your hand is uncomfortable, hold the food in any way that works for you. You just want to make it as easy as possible for your dog to get to the food. And protect your fingertips from nipping mouths.

You can sit down to play this if kneeling or bending down is not good for you. We do want to keep the food as low as possible so that we don't encourage them to jump up.

───────

FUNder

Concepts
Confidence/optimism, arousal up, focus, proximity.

What it does
I love this game for boosting your dog's love of proximity (being with you). You're teaching them that it's ok to go and interact with the environment, but it's also great fun to come back to you.

FUNder puts the FUN in going Under! It's a game that can be great to start having fun as soon as you get to the park. Does your dog want to dash away from you as soon as they're off the lead? FUNder is a great antidote for that.

It's a game that boosts confidence. Not all dogs will find it easy or natural to run between your legs and this game can help.

It's a great game with movement, but one where they have to think at the same time. They get to run around but still focus on being accurate to run between your legs.

How to play it
If you haven't played the **Orientation game** already – flick forward a few pages and play that first. FUNder takes Orientation game to another level.

Stand with your legs a little way apart. With your dog in front of you start to lure them in so that they know you have food and when they are between your legs throw the piece of food between your legs in the direction they are going.

Start by not throwing the food too far; you want your dog to be able to find the food easily. For a puppy or small dog, this might only be a foot (30cm) or so.

Larger, light-coloured, or smelly treats can help them locate the food quickly. Also playing on a hard surface like wood, tile or patio surface is easier to start with.

You want them to be able to get the food and eat it quickly so that you can mark it 'Yes!' just as they've eaten the food and started to lift their head.

Then you turn around to face them and repeat the step above.

As they get better at the game you can throw the food further or play on more challenging surfaces to find the food like grass. But ideally, you want them to locate the food quickly so that you can mark and get them bouncing back to you at speed!

Troubleshooting and variations
If they are struggling to follow or locate the food, play some more of the

games **Food Following**, **Paint the town red** and **Orientation game**.

If they are running around the outside of your legs, get them used to being in between your legs by just dropping some food in between your feet as they come in towards you. Over time, place the pieces of food ever so slightly further back so that they keep moving through your legs.

If you're unable to stand, you can play this going under a chair with open legs (if your dog isn't too big) or stick with **Orientation game** where you are throwing them from one side to the other, going past where you're seated. If your dog is too big to run between your legs, you can just get them running past you.

———

I love my name

Concepts
Proximity, engagement.

What it does
Recall is only recall if you can recall your dog back to you 100% of the time, no matter what is going on around them.

If you need to say "my dog's recall is fine unless..." there is another dog they want to play with / someone's picnic / some wildlife up a tree (insert as appropriate!).

This isn't recall.

I love my name game is the foundation game for recall, and a great starter for puppies so I wanted to include it here.

You want a dog whose eyes light up when you call their name and they come charging back to you!

How to play it
We want to build so much value into their name, they can't resist running back towards you.

Start by throwing a piece of food out, away from you. Using light coloured, larger pieces of food can help this game to start with. Your dog is likely to go and get the food and then they'll turn and look back at you to see if another piece is coming.

Just before they start to turn back towards you call their name or you can use something exciting like 'pup, pup, pup'! Reward them for coming back to you then throw the next piece of food out.

After repeating this several times, you can replace the 'pup, pup, pup' with their name.

You can increase desirability for the food (and therefore energy for the game) by lightly and briefly restraining them by a collar or harness, or hand on their chest if they are comfortable with this kind of contact from you.

Do this when they are with you as you throw the piece of food out.

Troubleshooting and variations
Just throw one piece of food out at a time to make it easier for your dog to locate it. It will also reduce the time they spend looking for food. If they do get into sniffing, don't nag them. Just wait it out and then add the 'pup, pup' or their name when they're lifting/turning their head and they are likely to come back to you. You can always add in a little **attraction noise** if you need to help them focus back on you.

Make the pieces of food fairly easy to chew so you don't have to wait too long for them to eat it! You want to try and get some speed into this game.

We tend to use our dog's name too much. For them to love hearing their name, we need to make sure we only use it positively and not too often. Otherwise, it can become 'white noise' or a predictor of something not so good. It's really important to try and not say their name in a negative way, either cross or nagging.

––––––

Middle

Concepts
Arousal up/arousal down, confidence/optimism, disengagement, engagement, flexibility, focus, proximity, self control/impulse control.

What it does
This is one of my all-time favourite games – it can do so much for you!

For dogs that struggle with **confidence**, being in the position of Middle can make them feel more confident because they have the physical presence of your legs around them. It also can help prevent other dogs from rushing up to yours because you are there. I think it also really helps you to feel more confident and in control, and if that's how you feel, your dog will sense that too.

It puts your dog in a great position to give you physical control. When I used to take Bodie to beginner agility, he would want to bounce around and try to greet other dogs. With him in Middle, I would get upward focus on me to look for the next piece of food plus he was physically easier to manage (he's 30kgs now) if he was getting bouncy.

For dogs that struggle with being handled, being in Middle can help them to feel more comfortable with being touched. Before I could run my hands down Bodie's legs easily at any other time, I could bend over and run my hand down his legs without him being concerned. (NB: Bending down does bring your face into closer contact with your dog's mouth or paws and claws if they were to jump up. Just something to be aware of.)

How to play it

The end position of the game is to have your dog between your legs facing forwards in the same direction as you. It doesn't matter whether they are in a **Stand** a **Sit** or a **Down**. We want to grow the cue 'middle' to mean come into this position and stay there no matter what is going on around us.

Step 1

Make sure your dog is comfortable between your legs; some dogs can struggle with this to start with, so don't worry if yours does too.

To make it clearer, I will describe what you do with your left and right hands. You can of course swap this around if this is more natural to you.

This first stage can mean you do a little bit of a dance! Have some food in your hands ready – one piece in your right hand, and several pieces in your left hand.

Stand with your legs slightly apart and bend forward to reach down between your legs with your right hand (your arm goes from front to back holding the one piece of food). If you can, try and reach through and around to the outside to lure your dog from the back to between your legs. Or you can do the little shuffling dance to keep repositioning yourself with your back to your dog and be quick to get the right hand through your legs until they follow the food through.

Some dogs find our backs quite challenging and will try and run round to keep your face in view. Keep at it and see how to adjust the way you move to help them end up in the right position to locate the tasty treat.

As soon as they are in between your legs, facing forwards use 2-3 pieces of the food from the left hand to feed them in that position.

Before they've had a chance to move out of position, give a release cue like 'break!' and throw a piece of food out a little way in front of them. We want to make sure they come out of the front, rather than backing out between our legs.

Repeat this a few times.

Step 2

Once your pup is finding it easier to get into position, we can start to build a desire for the release cue. We are trying to create some energy here.

Make sure they are in position, and we have fed them a few pieces of food in the Middle position. Then we build anticipation for the release cue by holding on to their collar or putting a hand lightly on their chest, as we throw the piece of food out in front of them. I like to create energy here by saying something like '3, 2, 1...Get it!' as I release them towards the food.

If your dog isn't trotting to get the food, ask a couple of things. Are they hungry enough? Is the food you're using tasty and desirable enough? Can you boost your energy in how you're playing it? It can just take time to build up.

You can turn around, so your back is facing them again, and repeat these steps a few times.

Step 3
Start to increase the angle that they are coming in at. So, rather than you turning around so that your back is facing them, stand so that they are a

slight angle to your side, but still slightly behind you. Repeat all the steps above.

You can also give the release cue to a piece of food that you drop out to the <u>side</u> of your foot, to help them carry on and head back round to come into Middle again.

This stage can take quite a while. Reward them lots when they do come in from more of an angle than they managed before.

Step 4
Continue to reduce the angle yet further until they are reliably coming from any angle and ending up in the Middle position.

Later stages
As they become more familiar with the game you can make the luring less obvious and add in the verbal cue 'middle' when they are reliably going into the end position. You can also make your cue a visual signal with your hand.

You can also release them onto a toy to help build up their control around things they want to go and interact with.

Troubleshooting and variations
If you have a big dog, you can play a version of this with your dog at your side. Or if you are feeling like a workout yourself you can play this with you in a squatting position to encourage your dog to come into the Middle position in a Down by crawling on their belly. This is hard work for both of you so keep the repetitions very low!

When your dog loves any game, it can become a reward in its own right. Middle is such a rewarding game for Bodie he'll happily play it, whether there is food involved or not and while I'm trying to get dressed!

You can layer games in with **Middle**. Here are a few ideas:

- You can do Puppy push-up (practise Sit, Down, Stand) on cue while in the Middle position.
- You can play **Magic hand** while they're in Middle.
- You can start to move around a little for **Middle on the move**.

––––––––

Noise box

Concepts
Confidence, flexibility, grit, independence, optimism, resilience.

What it does
I love games that are free and don't need any equipment. Your recycling box is often all you need. Noise box is a great confidence and independence boosting game, one to play before your recycling goes out.

Your dog will be making noises as they move things around with their nose and paws. Objects will be moving and touching their nose, head, and legs. This can help them be more confident with sounds generally and things they see moving out and about.

You can also set it up and leave them to it when they are confident, and you are happy they are safe. This can promote confidence and their sense of independence, as you step away and they are happily rooting out their breakfast while you get something else done.

How to play it
Start gently with a low sided box or bowl - whatever you have to hand. Ideally big enough so that your dog could stand in it with all four paws

and sides that are low enough so that it doesn't touch their belly/ribs as they step over the sides.

Place a couple of pieces of clean and safe recycling in it (e.g., plastic bottles, small cardboard boxes, scrunched up paper). Scatter some food around the outside to make sure your dog is comfortable with the object.

Encourage them to investigate as much as they are comfortable with.

If that's fairly easy, you can pop some food and/or toys in the box for them to forage for. Don't be tempted to put in too much, too soon. This is meant to be fun and easy for your pup to eat their breakfast and not an ordeal!

Do watch out to make sure they're not ingesting (eating) any of the cardboard, plastic etc. Ripping up is fine!
Play it a couple of times a week for confidence-boosting and helping with noise reactivity. Or just to keep them busy on a rainy day or when you need them occupied!

Troubleshooting and variations
You can hide a toy in there for them to find instead of food or ask them to find a toy by name if they know what it's called.

You can build up the difficulty as your dog becomes more confident and gritty! Place food inside boxes, cartons, and loo roll inners to layer up the challenge.

Metal and tin objects can also add an extra challenge for confident pups (make sure there are no sharp edges). As long as they're having fun, you can leave them to it.

———

Nose touch (hand targeting)

Concepts

Arousal down, calmness, confidence, engagement, focus, optimism, proximity, thinking in arousal.

What it does

I love this game for building close interactions between you and your dog. It helps your dog see more value in being near our hands.

Too often dogs can see our hands as not being the best things in the world. Our hands have to put a lead back on to stop them from running off in the park or take some amazing 'bin treasure' that they found out of their mouth, or put a collar and harness on them that they might not like at first.

It can help to bring your dog in closer to you on a walk. It can also help where dogs like to play 'keep away' when they see you get the lead ready to go home.

It's an easy game that you can play anywhere to get some focus on you. It's a super useful game that is the foundation for lots of other games – this is a game for everyone!

How to play it

I like to start this game sitting in a chair or on the ground if you can and it's appropriate for your dog. I would try to avoid leaning over your dog.

You can teach it in 2 ways. Method 1:

1. Start with holding each hand in a fist together in front of you, palms and folded knuckles are touching.
2. One of your hands is holding a treat ready.

3. Pop the empty hand out flat just to the side of your dog's nose – palm facing them.
4. Most dogs will sniff your palm – if they do, mark it with a 'yes!' and give them the treat from the other hand.
5. Repeat on the same side a couple of times and perhaps try the other side.
6. If they ignore the hand, curl it back into a fist with the other one or try popping it behind your back before popping it out again. Things can be more interesting if they disappear.
7. Add in the release cue – 'break!' and throw a piece of food away to get them moving.

Alternative method:

You can also present your hand out at your dog's head height and drop a piece of food into the hand as they come towards it. Mark it with a 'yes!' as they come towards the hand. They don't have to touch the hand to start with. They should come in to take the piece of food anyway. You can move your hand target around.

You can build up multiple touches and duration of holding the nose against your hand by not rewarding for the first brief touch but waiting for a repeat of the action or a little more pressure/time.

Troubleshooting and variations

Don't be tempted to move the 'target' hand back towards them to help.

The movement needs to come from them. If your dog gets stuck and looks at you confused, use your release cue to get them moving. Also, fold up the target palm. Only pop the flat palm out as they are trotting back towards you to encourage them to sniff it so that you can mark and reward something that looks closer to what you are looking for.

If your dog finds food very exciting and is getting over-excited by this game, play it with the lowest value food you have (dry food/kibble or vegetables perhaps?).

———

Novelty surprise party

Concepts
Confidence, flexibility, novelty, optimism.

What it does
There is a lot that life can throw at our dogs. Even if you got your puppy at 8 or 9 weeks old, you can't expose them to everything they'll face in their lives. But you can shape their brain at any age to be OK with new things that they might see or experience.

How to play it
This is a game to keep this calm and controlled. So, start with having your dog on a lead and not using any food.

You can set up a couple of objects from around your home, on the floor. Even though these are objects from your home, when you place them in the middle of the floor, our dogs can get worried by them. The location change can make the object novel and a little worrying for them.

You are going to let your dog move towards the objects if they are happy to. Don't lure them in with food at this stage because this can get them too focused on the food. When the food is gone they can suddenly realise they are somewhere they're scared of and this is not where we want them to be.

You've got them on the lead because you want this to be controlled. We don't want them to jump on something or run and knock into something and frighten themselves.

Watch their body language for any signs that they are not comfortable – some of the more obvious signs might be ears back, their weight staying over their back legs, clearly not wanting to approach the 'weird' object that isn't normally there.

Once they are happy with the objects, you can scatter a little food on the floor as you lead them around the objects. This encourages a little more interaction in this space with the novelty to make it a positive experience.

What is the response we want? No response at all! This is not about pushing them to go towards anything that scares them. Start with something easy and build it up over time.

Be imaginative with what you use for this one. I'd have this on my list of games to do at least once a month.

Troubleshooting and variations

For a very nervous dog, you may just be playing a game that they enjoy somewhere near the new objects. There shouldn't be any pressure to interact with the objects until you're confident that they are not going to be scared by it.

Nervous dogs don't always look nervous with ears pinned back, cowering away from things that worry them. Sometimes, they will just avoid certain things. Observe if there is anything that your dog is avoiding going closer to. Don't pressure them to go near it if they naturally don't want to. This is useful (but quite subtle) information for you.

You can build this up with all sorts of objects from around your home or garden. Think about objects that they know but put in a different way or position. For instance, an umbrella that is opened up, or a step ladder or ironing board laid flat on the floor. Even just moving a children's toy out of their room and placing it in the middle of the garden can make it novel.

Be aware of any sniffing, especially from male dogs – manage them before they decide to cock their leg on something!

Keep changing the objects to keep topping this one up. It can be surprising how confident dogs can suddenly get spooked by something. Also, senior dogs can struggle more as they age. Canine cognitive decline (dementia) is quite common as our dogs age, and this is a great game to boost their sense of optimism and help them not get startled by things they used to be fine with.

————

Orientation game

Concepts
Confidence, disengagement, engagement, focus, optimism, proximity.

What it does
Let's be honest, the environment is quite distracting for most of our dogs but we want them to be able to go and have a sniff and run around (and be a dog!). We also want them to come bouncing back to us when we want or need them to.

Orientation game builds up real value in them pinging straight back to you. It gets them excited as they start looking towards you and running towards you and it also helps to build their confidence in environments that they might otherwise find worrying.

If your dog isn't that into their food, it can also up their desire for the food as you make an experience out of it by bowling it along the floor and having fun hunting and finding the food.

I love to play this game with Bodie fairly early on when we get to a park. Once he's off the lead, it helps him have fun with us, making it less likely he wants to wander off and look for squirrels.

How to play it

It's good to play this game with food that is soft and fairly easy to chew quickly so that they are ready to come back to you for more, without having to stop and crunch for long!

Start playing this one inside at home or in the garden. Throw a piece of food out (just a little way to start with).
Wait for them to find and eat the food and just as they start to lift their head up, mark it with a bright 'yes!' and throw a piece of food out in another direction. You're not giving them the food reward for coming back to you.

The reward is the treat thrown away (i.e. to go back out into the environment) because they started to come back towards you.

Repeat a few times throwing the food out in different directions. Once your dog gets used to this game, they can start to bounce back towards you ready for the next release out again.

Like most games, the timing of your marker ('yes!') and throwing of the food is key. Time it just as they are starting to lift their head up to see what's happening next. If their head is down and sniffing, they are more likely to ignore you. We want to give them the best chance of getting it right!

Troubleshooting and variations

If your dog is struggling to follow the food, play the **Food following** game to help. If they are struggling to find the food, don't throw it as far, play it on a hard surface (not grass) and play it with larger, pale or smelly pieces of food.

Don't nag them when they're locating the piece of food. Wait for them to find it (or go and help them look for it). You can make a little **attraction noise** if they need some encouragement to start coming back towards you.

If they get very distracted, start playing this one somewhere really easy like a room with a hard floor.

Once your dog is used to playing this game, you can take it out and about, when you're ready. Don't forget a longline is a great way to give your dog some freedom, while still giving you control if they didn't manage to make the best choice when something too distracting caught their eye.

――――――

Paint the town red

Concepts
Arousal up, confidence, engagement, focus, grit, optimism, proximity.

What it does
Paint the town red builds on the **Food following** game. We are now increasing their drive to stay connected with our hand. This game boosts their drive and desire to play games with food. And have fun, wherever you are.

How to play it
Follow the steps for **Food following** as a warm-up.

This time imagine that your hand is a paint brush and you have dipped your fingers into a pot of red paint.

You are going to paint the floor red with just the back of your hand. Make slow, sweeping movements (imagine a figure of 8 on the floor in front of you) keeping your palm facing your dog's nose at all times (rotation is coming from your shoulder if that's comfortable for you).

Keep your hand low enough so that it is easy for them to take the food without stretching their neck up too high.

Let them get the piece of food in your hand, then reload to go again.

Start to increase the speed of the figure of 8 movements.
When your hand gets to the top or the bottom of the '8' you can flick your hand back round to try and create more drive and desire to get the piece of food.

You can celebrate when they get the piece of food to increase desire and awareness that they did a great job!

We want them to be 'winning' this game with real ease to start with. This is not about overly testing them. We can grow the difficulty once they're having fun with it.

You can then start to take a step or two forwards or backwards to increase the distance that your hand is travelling, and your dog is moving to follow the food. If you lose their nose from the palm of your hand (you should be able to feel a wet nose most of the time), slow it down a little to make sure they can stay connected with you. You're not trying to trick them or hide the food, just increase their desire to get the food that is in your palm.

Troubleshooting and variations
If your pup isn't staying with you, slow your hand down.

Keep close to your dog's nose so that they don't lose their way and stop following. We want them to think they're always just about to get the food – because they are!

If they don't seem very motivated, try with higher value food. Or go back to playing **Food following** for a while longer.

If you have a bigger dog or a dog without a really flexible spine, keep your hand movements bigger, taking a step or two to make the size of the figure of 8 motion comfortable for them.

———

Toy switch

Concepts
Confidence, disengagement, engagement, optimism, thinking in arousal.

What it does

We want our dogs to choose us over anything else that is going on around them, every time! This game teaches our dogs that whatever we're doing, is more fun than other choices they could make.

It's also a great foundation for puppies to get used to letting go of something and getting something else cool in return. This can make 'drop' or 'out' much easier, which is important for getting something out of their mouths if you need to.

This game is also a foundation that you can use for growing a retrieve. We want our dog to want to play with us, no matter what else is on offer.

How to play it

To start with, ideally, you'll have two toys that are the same or are very similar in value to your pup. They also need to be big enough for you to hold and your dog to be able to grip (so not great with tennis balls).

Simply start playing a game with one of the toys. Get a good game going! A bit of tug is great but play in a way that your pup enjoys.

If your dog isn't that comfortable being close to you, this game can be a good way to reinforce them being near you. When you're playing, they will be naturally drawn into you while they're having fun. Just make sure not to crowd them or bend over them, which could make the experience too much for them.

Troubleshooting and variations

If your dog wants to run off with the toy that they have, you really need to up your energy to make the toy that you have irresistible! Try tapping or banging it on the floor (as long as this doesn't worry them) or making fun noises (higher pitched normally worked better) and really animate your toy. This is not a time to hold back and feel shy! Play like no one is watching!

If your dog doesn't want to let go of the toy that they have, you need to immobilise it to make it less appealing. Put your hand on it firmly, or a foot or a knee as you animate the other toy. Your toy will become more attractive if they are identical toys. Once you have hold of it you can 'hide' it under your arm/armpit.

If your dog is not that play-driven, you can increase their love of play over time. Don't feel pressured to try and make them do something that they're not ready for.

Look at what they chose to do when they're having fun.

Do they pounce on things or like to chase or catch things, or parade around with something in their mouth? Try and pair something that they absolutely love into a game with you. The value of doing something they love spreads onto you.

Don't worry if you don't have two identical toys. Be resourceful. Can you use two old socks? Perhaps with a tennis ball tied into the toe of each one? Or a couple of kitchen towel cardboard inners?

You can build up the difficulty of this game by using different value toys.

13

HELP - I NEED STRUCTURE

Even when you know what to do, how hard is it to stay motivated all of the time?

I know how to eat healthily but still I lose my way and resort to quick and unhealthy options all too often.

Even if you know quite a few training games to play with your puppy or dog, how often do you find yourself playing the same games all the time? I still find myself doing this with Bodie, despite being a dog trainer! So I wanted to come up with a simple planner to help me play the right games to really make progress with the behaviour struggles we were having with him.

I designed the Pup Talk Training Tracker to give structure, the right focus and motivation to keep going and keep changing things up.

20% of our time can get 80% of the results you want (the Pareto's principle). Let's really focus on finding the right 20%!

I think the motivation to keep doing things can be really hard. When we do something early on, we are all excited and energetic about it. But then we get a bit bored and forget the initial excitement. Or it gets tough going and we don't feel like we're making much progress.

But the phrase 'no progression is regression' is so true when it comes to our dogs. You can find that they go backwards with some behaviours if you don't keep topping them up. Have you found your dog starting to react to noises that they didn't use to? Or the occasional bark at a dog is now being something they do more often? Or is their recall getting worse when it used to be really reliable?

Consistency is also something that plays a big part in our dog's behaviour. Even if we are being consistent with our dogs, what about other people that live with them and come into contact with them? It is very easy to be giving our dogs mixed messages so that it's not really a surprise they don't behave consistently.

The Training Tracker also helps people answer questions like:

- How many times a week should I be training with my pup?
- When should I be training?
- How do I know what to focus on first?
- I work all sorts of hours, how can I fit in training my pup around a crazy household?

If you want to use the Pup Talk Training Tracker, you can get 50% off by using the code THEBOOK50

here www.pup-talk.mykajabi.com/pup-talk-training-tracker

At the time of publishing, you can also choose to add on a live interactive group coaching session with me to work out the games you need for your pup's specific struggles. I limit these to 8 people per 90-minute session to make sure everyone goes away with a plan.

You could also design your own training plan by grabbing a notebook or a sheet of paper and following these steps:

1. Make two columns. In the first column write down the biggest struggles you are having with your dog. Ask other people if relevant - in the household, a dog walker, doggy daycare etc. You can review these after a month to see what's changed.

2. Think about the concept that will help each of these struggles - it helps to imagine the opposite of what the struggle is. You can have more than one concept for any of the struggles. Write these down in the second column.
If you need to, revisit Chapter 3 for help with concepts. If you're still struggling with this, you might want to join a live workshop coaching session to help with this. There's a booking link with the online Training Tracker at https://pup-talk.mykajabi.com/pup-talk-training-tracker

3. In the first column, highlight the three struggles that will have the biggest impact for both of you. From the corresponding concepts that appear most often, pick just three.

4. For each of these three concepts write down some games that will help. If you're struggling, or you need more game ideas, you may want to join Pup Talk The Pack, or book a 1-2-1 with me. Or you could sign up to the Absolute Dogs Training Academy when the doors are open.

5. It can help to add a note alongside each game:

   H - great games to play at home.
   W - games to play on walks, in the park etc.
   N - new games - best to be played at home and with lots of tasty rewards/favourite toys.

6. The weekly section of the Training Tracker is set out like this:

	AM	PM	AD HOC
Monday			
Tuesday			
Wednesday			
Thursday			
Friday			
Saturday			
Sunday			
Notes			

Fill out games into the AM/PM/Ad Hoc boxes. Think about when you have more time for your dog. If you go on walks, when will you be taking them out? When do you need them to relax because you'll be busy?

7. Some games benefit from being played daily. Get these mapped in.

8. Don't forget to add in daily passive calming activities (if you need some new ideas – check out Chapter 5).

9. Then add in some fun stuff - whatever you fancy, perhaps trying a new game once a month.

10. Keep it somewhere handy to tick games off as you go, especially if more than one person is involved in the training games. Consistency is so helpful for faster learning.

11. Make a note of any wins (big and small), struggles and events of note. You can use this to prioritise the concepts and games for the following week. Identifying patterns can be really helpful. You can also look back to see longer-term progress when you feel like you're not moving forwards. This is so helpful for motivation.

12. Don't worry about following the plan to the letter - it's a guide to give some structure. But no beating yourself up when you need to vary it or didn't tick everything off!

13. Accept you can't do everything at once. Be kind to yourself if it doesn't feel like it's going to plan, or you take a step or two backwards. This is so normal. Progress (over weeks and months) and not perfection is what we're looking for.

14. If you have more than one dog, complete a new tracker for each one. They will probably look quite different.

15. At the end of the week, fill out a new week. The new week can look very similar to the previous one, although you might want to add in one new game to mix it up a little. Or schedule less if you found it too much.

You can use this simple system whenever you feel like your training has stalled. Or you feel like your dog's behaviour is going backwards. Or there has been a big life change or event that has had an impact on you or your dog. Have a fresh look at their struggles and the concepts that you'd like to grow that will help them.

14

CHALLENGES AND WHAT CAN DERAIL YOU

Having a dog isn't always easy. Or should that be - often isn't easy? Even if everything stays the same in your dog's life.

Let's face it if you've got a naturally chilled-out dog (like Fergus the wonderful Westie) you're probably not reading this book!

It is so common for my clients to be close to (or in) tears at times. It can feel lonely. It can feel like you're not making any progress. It can make you feel cross, guilty, overwhelmed, lonely or frustrated. It can feel like yours is not the right home for your dog. It can feel like you're failing them.

I've been through this with Bodie. For the first 18 months we had him, he was particularly challenging, and I went through many emotions when we were having difficult days.

Nothing stays the same

There are lots of challenges that we can face as dog owners/guardians.

Puppies are obviously a handful (although often much more so than people thought). And then just as you get through the worst of toilet training, sleepless nights, and biting, then you have hormones to deal with. The adolescent (or teenage) phase in dogs can bring real challenges. Does it feel like they'll listen to other people, but test their boundaries with you? Or that they seem to forget a lot of what they learned as a puppy? There is research that backs this up. If you're going through this right now, try and take some comfort from knowing that it will pass and training games will help you through it.

Even once you're past the adolescent phase, and your dog is considered an adult, all sorts of life events can have an impact on your dog and its behaviour. This could be changes in their environment and the people around them. Perhaps you need to move home or have some building works done. Even something as simple as a new kitchen appliance being fitted can be a challenge for some dogs.

Perhaps there are new human additions to the family (babies, children, or adults) Maybe some of the people move out or there are new dogs or animals added to the home, or perhaps an animal passed away – or maybe something significant happened that can trigger changes in your dog. Unfortunately, some dogs get attacked by other dogs or they can get frightened by a sudden loud noise, or it can be a series of things that you don't really notice. But left unaddressed, your dog becomes more and more reactive to things in their environment.

There can be medical factors that influence your dog's behaviour. Perhaps increasing pain from stiffness and arthritis or an undiagnosed injury, illness, or skin condition and then there is old age. Canine cognitive decline means structural changes in our dogs' brains, which affects their behaviour and sometimes we will never know the cause of the change in their behaviour.

What about your expectations?

What did you think it would be like getting your dog? What did you imagine? Cuddles with your dog and relaxed walks in the woods, with them off-lead and trotting around at your side? Or curled up with their head in your lap as you binge on a new Netflix series?

Is the reality a bit different to the dream that you had?

What about the people around you?

There are doubters all around us! What we know about dogs is growing all the time. There are lots of differences of opinion and there are lots of differing training methods.

If you have picked the route of positive-rewards, games-based, no 'aversives' training you will probably come up against people that have differing views and they probably won't be afraid to tell you where you are going wrong.

I know it can be challenging to deal with the doubters, but always come back to what you feel is right for you and your dog. What is your gut telling you about what you need to do to build the best relationship with your dog?

If the doubters are in your household this can be really challenging because you want consistency for your dog. My advice is to do what you can. Lead by example. Share your knowledge where it feels right. Trust that, in time, your dog will show that what you are doing works. It's a beautiful thing when the doubters see the results you are getting and start playing games with your dog as well!

You need support

Try to surround yourself with people that think like you and can support you. You can gain strength from knowing that you are not alone in the struggles you're having. Seeing other people having successes can help to lift you and help you keep going. This might be online in supportive Facebook communities.

If you're not already, I'd love you to join us in one of the friendliest Facebook communities of dog lovers www.facebook.com/groups/puptalk/ -

you never need to feel alone.

Or following social media accounts that share your struggles and are positively working towards calm and happy dogs. Are you following me on Instagram? @puptalk101

As for handling the doubters around you? For me, the best way can be to just quietly get on with doing things the way you want to. Once people start seeing you playing games and the results that will come with it, they can get more intrigued and start picking up some of the things you do with your dog.

Before you know it, your partner or children may be playing FUNder instead of just chucking a ball around!

Knowledge gives you confidence

You may come up against unhelpful comments and unhelpful people. Some people are just not open-minded to modern, relationship-building training methods. My approach is to thank them for their opinions and say it's great people have their views and just move on.

Hold on tight to your belief that the way you are doing it is right for you and your dog. When you tell people why you want to ditch the walks, some people are going to be surprised, maybe critical. But were you 100% convinced about it when you first read the title of this book? Perhaps not. But hopefully, I have put across a convincing argument if you have got this far. At least enough for you to want to try it.

Learning a bit more about modern dog training can give you the confidence to help tackle the doubters of your approach to your dog (if you want to spread the word). A big high five for reading this book!

To give you a little science in an easily digestible read, I love Alexandra Semyonova's book *The 100 Silliest Things People Say About Dogs*. She beautifully debunks myths AND gives you the understandable science to back it up.

What about the setbacks?

Setbacks can derail you. You felt like you were making some progress and then BAM! Something happens and you feel like you're right back at square one.

Perhaps you'd stopped taking your dog outside for walks and had been working on a great training plan at home. They seemed so much better, and you introduced some short walks in quieter places and then you came across a dog that was too close and your dog is a barking and lunging mess again.

Sometimes you need to test things to see what's changed. This isn't a failure on your part or your dog. This is giving you some really useful information. It's telling you that they're not quite ready for that situation yet. Don't beat yourself up, just go back a stage or two and keep helping them grow the skills they need.

Even if you don't have a big setback, it can feel like you're not making much progress. Or you're not making progress fast enough. Or you feel like you're going backwards. All of this is really normal. Our dogs are animals. Progress is rarely in a straight line. Who wants a robot dog anyway?

My quick tips to help get through these times:

- Take a break from training. Perhaps a few days, perhaps not playing the games you've been working hard on. When you come back to a game after taking a break, they can suddenly jump forwards.
- Try doing less. We can put too much pressure on ourselves and our dogs. Maybe go back to some easy basic games.
- Just play some games for the fun of it. Think about doing nothing more than activities that will build your relationship. Hand feeding them something tasty? Being in the garden while

they chew on a tasty natural chew? A fun game of tug with no structure?

- Do you need to do a little more? Be honest, could you step it up a little?
- Try something different.
- Get some support from the right friends and/or family. Tell them how you're struggling.
- Get some informed or professional help. Sometimes a small tweak to what you're doing can make a massive difference.
- Be kind to yourself! You ARE doing the best you can.
- Drink some water; if you're hydrated, you'll feel better and make better decisions. Or have a glass of wine/gin and tonic/tea etc and breathe...

Your mindset is so important. You can do this!

PART 3

15

QUICK TRAINING TIPS

I wanted to give you a bonus chapter compiling some of my favourite training tips into one place. There are also some great training foundations covered here. These apply to so many situations and struggles with our dogs.

Many of these nuggets of training gold I have learned from Lauren Langman and Tom Mitchell from Absolute Dogs and my other fellow Pro Dog Trainers.

There is intentional repetition from the rest of the book.

"Repetition is the mother of learning..."

ZIG ZIGLAR

Attraction noise

We tend to use our pups' names far too much and if we're honest, probably not always positively. Who remembers "Fenton!...FENTON!!" as the dog shot off chasing deer in Richmond Park.

We want our dog's eyes to sparkle when we call their name and have them come rushing over to us. They won't do this if they hear their name too much or if we nag them or tell them off while using it. "Rex...leave it!... REX...COME HERE!!". It just becomes 'white noise.'

Using an attraction noise can be really useful to help your pup know to look at you or come in closer to you. I love a 'kiss kiss' noise. Some people love a horsey style 'click click'. Some people (yes Tom and Lauren) have a great shrill 'brrrrup' noise that I can't even spell let alone make!

Pick what feels natural for you, make the noise and reward your pup for looking at you when you make the noise. Practise it when there isn't much to get distracted by. Noise – reward. Noise – reward and then build it up when they're slightly further away or a little more into whatever they are investigating.

Save their name for special occasions, like the shoes that you can only wear when you're getting a taxi to and from a restaurant and sitting down for most of the evening.

Build it lots, test it little

Build value in **proximity** before testing their recall. Build up their ability to be **calm** before putting them in situations that might get them over-excited. Grow their **confidence** before you put them in a situation that tests them.

Challenges all around you? Look at every challenge as a training opportunity

If they are barking at something in the garden, this gives you a chance to practise **DMT**. If your dog is pulling on the lead, this is a great opportunity to practise **Figure of 8 walking**.

Try not to feel frustrated when you are facing a challenging situation with your dog. Take a breath, drop those shoulders, and play a game! Or manage the situation by going home or going somewhere else.

Did you know…? Tomato ketchup can neutralise the smell of poo

If your dog has rolled in poo, this is a useful one! Wipe some ketchup on the offending area and wash or wipe off thoroughly.

Be aware, ketchup can leave a white dog tinged with pink for a little while. Which is worse though? I keep a sachet in the car for emergencies.

Ditch the bowl if you haven't already

If you deliver an 'experience' with food, you can do so much. The reward is not the food you're giving them, it's the experience you're delivering that makes all the difference.

Is your dog not very motivated by their dry food/kibble? Try mixing it with some tasty and smelly food and store it in pots in the fridge ready to go. The dry food takes on some of the smell and flavour. Strong cheese or hot dog can work well if that's right for your dog.

Dogs don't speak English (or any other language)

We tend to forget that dogs don't understand any spoken language. Until we teach them that a particular sound (a word) means do something. We need to pair the word with the action as they are doing it (or just before they do it).

To do this, you need to focus on getting the reliable action you want first; add the word later on. They need to learn the action <u>before</u> we put a cue on it.

Enjoy training with your dog

Playing training games should never feel like hard work. It should always be fun for you and your dog.

Forget perfect - practice makes progress

Perfect doesn't exist! Just keep on going in the right general direction.

We want progress, but training isn't a straight line. Sometimes it can feel like you're going backwards. This is when you need to keep going. The next mini 'win' is just around the corner.

Please note this does not mean you should be doing long training sessions – see Less is always more below.

Itching - dogs shouldn't be scratching more than once or twice a day

If your dog itches more than once or twice a day, you have an 'itchy dog'. You should investigate what the cause might be and what you can do to help.

Itching and scratching can also be a stress behaviour, so if your vet clears them of medical issues, then they need more easy training wins and fewer challenges.

Itching regularly can fill up their 'bucket' and make any behaviour struggles worse.

Less is always more

Keep training game sessions super short to maximise the learning and the fun. It's better to play a game for 2-3 minutes and leave them wanting more. Even less for puppies. Neither of you should have the chance to get bored.

It's also better to do 2-5 repetitions that are precisely rewarded than playing a game for too long and they seem to get worse at it.

A quick game or two is really easy to fit in and around your day which means you have no excuse for not playing with your dog!

Long lines - don't be afraid to use a long line or training line for many months (even years)

Long lines are a fabulous tool to help stop your dog from making mistakes. Do put knots in your long line about one metre apart. This means you can stand on it to stop them if they're running off and the next knot will stop under your foot (unless you're wearing flipflops).

Please don't try and hold it in your hands. I know too many people that have broken fingers and lost skin from trying to hold on to the line when a dog is on the move!

Once you've got used to handling a long line, it is much more training friendly than the extending leads. You have a lot more control. Channel your inner cowboy and practise with one.

Mark (marker words) and reward tips

Don't keep repeating your marker. Once is enough, just make it precise as to when you use it.

Try to avoid giving the food reward and then following it up with a fuss, unless your dog genuinely finds this rewarding. I see quite a few dogs shy away from this.

I suggest avoiding using your dog's name as a marker. If we use their name less frequently, it has more effect. Get used to not saying it if you can.

Your pup doesn't need a big fuss and lots of 'there's a good boy' every time they work out what you wanted them to do. But they do need to know that that specific thing they just did, is what you are rewarding so that they can do it again.

No progression is regression

We need to keep topping up our dogs' skills to cope with everything that modern life throws at them. We can do this with fun and simple games. The world is training your dog if you don't, so do something small every day.

Praise - always praise your dog when they come back to you

Even if it took them a long time, or you don't like what they did before coming back! If you tell them off, they are going to be even less likely to come back swiftly next time.

Relationship is everything - think about the relationship you have with your pup like a bank account

How much positivity are we paying into the relationship bank account? How much are we taking out?

Our relationship with our pup is so fundamental to working together. We want them to work with us because they enjoy it. Not because we are making them do something. Playing games with your dog is a great way to grow your relationship with them and boost their training.

If you have an adolescent dog, focusing on your relationship with them is even more vital. Research shows that 'teenage' dogs are programmed to test the boundaries with us as their guardians. It can be quite a challenging time. So, even when it feels like their behaviours are regressing, focussing on fun, no-pressure relationship building games can help you get through this phase.

Sniffing bums is normal!

It's like us shaking hands with someone. If you pull your dog away, you can make them look rude. It gives them lots of valuable information, so don't be embarrassed about it. A quick nose to nose greeting, and then a butt sniff, before moving on, is very polite.

Start the day right

It's so useful to start your dog's day with what they need more of. It helps them understand what their job is for the day. If they need more **calmness**, how about a lick mat as part of their breakfast? If they need more **optimism** or **confidence**, how about a **Noise box** for breakfast? If they need more independence, how about a stuffed Kong in their crate while the rest of the household is getting ready?

Start a training session with an easy game that they know and love

We call this a 'conversation starter'. It might be a quick game of tug and let them 'win' it. Or **FUNder**, **Orientation**, **Two paws on** - what does your dog love? It gets them in the right headspace to tackle something harder.

Train FOR the situation not IN the situation

A lot of traditional dog training involves training with our dogs when something is happening, i.e. IN the situation.

Training FOR the situation means giving your dog the skills they need before you put them in a situation where they need those skills. This is one of the fundamental reasons for ditching the walks.

Train the dog in front of you

Don't get hung up on labels for types or breeds of dogs. Yes, there are breed traits; terriers are likely to do this, herding breeds do that etc. Yes, it is useful information, but all dogs are different. Appreciate what makes them different. Don't get hung up on comparing your dog to anyone else's; even from the same litter.

Also, dogs can be different from day to day. If you think they've had a stressful day, make the following day or two an opportunity to empty their bucket. Listen to and trust your intuition.

Training is always happening, even when you're not 'training'

When you get your treat pouch out, and the lead and toys come out, training is happening. But training is happening constantly. Try and be conscious of what they're learning all the time when we are not 'training'.

Don't let them rehearse behaviours you don't want. Think about any of these (and others) that they might be doing:

- Running off with a toy.
- Pulling on a lead.
- Barking at the window.
- Playing boisterously with other dogs.

Manage whatever it is so they can't rehearse it. If they get to rehearse it, they will get better at it!

Treats - make your treats go as far as possible

Chop food up small for most games, unless you need the food to be found more easily. You get lots more opportunities to reward and reinforce good decisions. Your dog won't feel any less rewarded if a piece of food is smaller. You can keep larger, paler pieces of food for games where they need to locate the food quickly and easily.

Yawning and scratching

Do you notice your dog yawning in training or other situations? Or suddenly sit down and scratch, at what seems like a random moment? They could be feeling pressured to do something or they are confused and are not sure what to do. Perhaps get them moving or make whatever you are asking them to do a little easier.

And last, but absolutely not least...

Don't be afraid to ditch the walks

If more than 50% of your walks are not good experiences for you and your dog, you are constantly topping up their stress/excitement bucket to overflowing. This just isn't helpful. Swap your walks for activities at home.

16

HOW TO RESTART TRADITIONAL 'WALKS'

If you have stopped walking your dog for any reason (or you haven't started walking them because they are a puppy, or any other reason) when and how do you start?

Grow a new circuit

Remember a walk is just a circuit (Chapter 1) You can take the games you've been playing and play them in different places. We want to stretch our dogs a little, but not too much so that they can't cope. You don't need to just jump straight into a traditional 'walk'.

If you haven't already, play the games in different areas in your home – kitchen, living room, a bedroom? And don't forget the less common places like a bathroom, utility room or hallway. Of course, play them in a garden or on a balcony if you have one.

The front doors to our homes are often a cause of excitement or worry with people and packages coming and going. You can start playing games near the front door (with the door closed). Then with the door open (with a lead or longline on if you need to for safety).

Think about what else can be small steps in growing the 'circuit':

- Outside your front door.
- In your garage.
- On your driveway.
- In your front garden.
- Around your car.
- In your car.
- Out of the front gate and straight back in.
- A few meters along the pavement and back again.
- A drive straight to a quiet shopping centre car park.
- Do you have a friend's garden that you can use?
- Can you hire an enclosed field where you are confident of what your dog will be exposed to?

Be creative with the spaces you take the training games to. Don't feel you have to jump straight into the traditional walk.

To make a plan to build up these layers of difficulty, it might be useful to use the training tracker method I cover in Chapter 13. Add in notes of the different places where you want to play the games that week.

This is a really important step in helping your dog to be able to take the skills they've learned and apply them in lots of different places. If your dog struggled in the park before, don't be tempted to try and take a game from your living room straight into a park to see if things have got better. Grow those new skills, little by little, in slightly more testing environments.

Create your own version of a walk, where your dog only gets to behave in a way that you absolutely love. Perhaps this is them trotting calmly along at your side, with them looking up at you every now and again. Imagine it now... You can make this a reality.

Changing the picture

It might sound unlikely, but we can use a different piece of equipment to change how our dog feels on a walk. We are 'changing the picture' for them. This could be a different type of harness, or a head collar, or a jacket. Be flexible!

Dogs are masters of predicting, and by changing something that feels physically different, we can change their expectations of what's to come, to help get them into a different headspace. You can change at least one of the predictors of previously stressful experiences.

A note about head collars

For me, head collars are absolutely not about having physical control of a dog's nose and head. But, in addition to changing the picture for your dog, it can have a positive effect on you by helping you feel more confident. Especially if your dog has managed to pull you over onto your face or damage a finger. When you feel like you have more control, you can be calmer, and your dog will feel calmer and less likely to react. Making a lovely positive cycle.

Imagine if your dog only had positive experiences when wearing its new head collar (or other piece of equipment). If you play the games at home with the head collar on with tasty rewards. If you only create little circuits that your dog nails every time. Over time, they will associate only positive experiences with the wearing of the head collar, helping them to transition to experiences that they used to find a little more challenging.

We absolutely must positively introduce the new equipment. See Chapter 12 and look up the **Cone** game. We want our dog's eyes to light up when we pull out this new piece of equipment. When I pick up Bodie's head collar, he instantly thinks 'sausages'!

You want to play lots of **Cone** game with a cone, yoghurt pots, beakers, the head collar or harness or coat. Get to the stage of them diving to get their head through it or in it. Only then would I start using it in combination with the steps above or growing a circuit.

Read about how introducing a head collar really helped Gayle with Ella in Chapter 17.

When do you know you're ready?

Knowing exactly when you're ready isn't always easy. If your dog is nervous or reactive especially, I would say don't be in a rush. But you can test it little by little with some of the steps above.

Pick the games you know they know and love. Stretch them a little with baby steps. If they struggle to concentrate in any of these areas, maybe they're not quite ready for that step just yet. Practise a little more in the locations they can manage and then try again somewhere a little more testing again when you feel ready.

Remember when you make the games more difficult by changing the environment, you can step up the value of the reward to help their motivation. A game Bodie will happily play for kibble in the back garden may well need some hot dog or chicken for a park with other dogs in it.

If your dog is coming back to activity after illness or injury, please follow the advice of your veterinarian. Short periods of road walking are likely to be advised to rebuild your dog's fitness.

Trust yourself and your dog

Don't be afraid to test and stretch them a little. If we don't, they won't be able to progress. Sometimes they may have made lots of progress and we won't know if we don't put them in a new situation and if there is too much of a reaction, you can always step down the difficulty again for a few days or weeks and try again when you feel ready.

Don't worry if you try something and it doesn't go to plan. Everything you have done, to this point, won't be broken. Just take this as useful information as to where your dog is at right now and keep working within areas they can cope with and pat yourself on the back for trying.

Don't be tempted to 'push through' a struggle if your dog isn't making great choices. We want to make sure they don't get the opportunity to keep rehearsing the choices we don't want (pulling on the lead, lunging, barking etc.). If it happens now and again, it's not a big deal but we want to make sure they don't fall back into old habits.

Celebrate every little win along the way. No matter how small. Appreciate anything that looks like a little bit of progress.

Please try not to feel pressured to walk your dog. To reiterate what I've already covered you are not 'being mean' to your dog by not rushing back to taking them out for walks. You are helping them have a less stressful life while helping them grow the skills they need to calmly enjoy other spaces in the future. Hold firm in the face of outside pressure and listen to what your gut tells you (as long as your gut is being nice to you!).

17

ONE REAL LIFE STORY

I learned about the concept and importance of 'ditching the walks' from my Pro Dog Trainer development with Absolute Dogs. But what really inspired me to write a specific book about it has been my clients.

Some of my clients have had very real struggles. From puppies that 'go on strike' (bum plonked firmly on the floor and not wanting to budge), to over-excited dogs that were jumping up and dragging their humans down the street. There have been the dogs that are so nervous of things outside the home that their 'buckets' were completely over-flowing all the time.

I want to thank all of my clients for trusting me and putting the training plans into practice and trusting themselves to take, what many people see as, a bold or unusual step.

When talking about dogs with training issues, how many times have you heard people say something like this?

"Just give them more exercise."

"You just need to tire them out."

Hopefully, you are as converted as I am to the reasons why this does not work.

I'd like to specifically mention one of my clients...

Gayle and Ella the 18 month-old Border Collie

I love this case study because there are so many small changes Gayle implemented that work together to create real change. Life was pretty challenging for both Gayle and Ella.

Ella the Border Collie was 18 months old when Gayle and I put a new training plan together. Ella was really struggling with hyper-vigilance (noticing every noise and movement), very noise sensitive (terrified of loud bangs and even scared of distant traffic noises), very fearful of horses, animals (even on the TV), she struggled with recall around any distractions and Ella pulled poor Gayle right over more than once.

She was so fearful; at times she would drop and flatten to the floor and wouldn't move. Gayle was an experienced Collie owner and tried so hard to find quiet spaces to walk with Ella. But none of the walks were a positive experience for either of them. Gayle was, understandably, finding it distressing and was wondering if they were the right home for Ella.

Ella also wasn't really into her food, meaning rewarding her wasn't straightforward. Often she would be too stressed to eat.

I'm writing this chapter, four months after Gayle ditched nearly all of their walks. Yes, there is still work to do, but there has already been some great progress to report.

With none of their walks being a completely positive experience, these needed to stop.

Gayle also stopped taking Ella to doggy daycare. She found it so over-stimulating, she was exhausted afterwards. This wasn't adding anything to the relationship Gayle was trying to grow with her.

We worked through a plan to replace the walks with games at home. And build up Ella's **confidence** and **optimism**, along with the ability to **disengage** from things and be comfortable with **novelty**.

They started off playing the games just at home and then took them out to their yard. Over time, Gayle took the games out to a quiet grassy back alley. She used a long line to make sure Ella couldn't make any poor decisions! Ella loves her ball, so Gayle used this for a few games as a fun reward in the new spaces.

Ella grew in **confidence** little by little, until she would eventually walk happily to the end of the alley. I love how slowly Gayle took these steps. Often, we are so keen to go back to a 'proper walk' or to see if our dogs have made a big improvement. But the baby steps (no matter how small or how slow they can feel) are so vital to keep making progress without any significant setbacks.

A big turning point has been Ella being able to keep moving, rather than dropping into a 'pancake' and not wanting to move. Stillness means her body isn't helping her brain. Movement is so helpful in allowing dogs to work through their struggles. You often see dogs 'shake it off' after an event as they help themselves to 'reset'.

Gayle also found it helpful to use a head collar. Some of the time you can 'change the picture' by positively introducing a new piece of equipment that feels different on their body. It also helped Gayle to feel more confident that Ella wouldn't pull her over, and Ella would have picked up on this and relaxed more as well.

After a few months, Ella started to be able to listen more to Gayle. The relationship had been growing steadily. Plus, when Ella is calmer, she is more able to listen. Gayle still lets Ella decide when she's out, what she feels comfortable with. If she's not enjoying the experience, Gayle ends the walk early and comes home. She still uses the quiet alley to play games. There is never any pressure to go out for 'a walk.'

Ella can now relax more because she knows she can rely on Gayle not to put her in situations that she doesn't feel comfortable in. Gayle can give her a reassuring 'come on, walk walk' and Ella can get moving again. The growth in the trust between them is wonderful.

Ella is now fine when Gayle is out at work. The neighbours don't report any barking and Gayle can see her, on the monitor, mostly settled until she gets home at lunchtime. Even though Ella does now go out for walks, there is no lunchtime walk, just some quick games in and around the home and a tasty Kong to settle back down for the afternoon.

They didn't used to be able to watch TV programmes with animals on and now, with a little gentle encouragement into 'Middle' and a calming stroke, Ella recently managed to watch a whole programme on foxes!

There have even been a couple of holiday breaks away where Ella was able to sit calmly under a pub garden table. Even being approached by the odd friendly person for a little fuss. This was unthinkable a few months ago as she would be too excitable and get a bit snappy.

Ella also still pulls some of the time, partly through over-excitement and sometimes when she's worried by a sudden noise like a big bang. And recall is also a work in progress. But she's not even two years old yet. There is plenty of time; training is a fun part of owning a dog, not something to be ticked off a to-do list as done!

It's been amazing to see the time and patience Gayle has given Ella, to help her become a calmer and more confident girl and it feels like this is just the start of how much they can achieve together.

When I caught up with Gayle, she said "And then all of a sudden, she wasn't so scared. It can still be really hard sometimes, but I can tell when Ella's bucket is full, and I know what to do. We can now go exploring nice new quiet spots at the weekend."

Gayle was very open at the start about how she seriously doubted that they were the right family for Ella. It was a very challenging time, but she now says, "I'm so glad she ended up with us."

And I couldn't be more delighted for them.

Training pull-outs:

- Ditch the walks for a sustained period and replace them with games to build up new skills.
- You spend less time playing games than you would have spent walking (less is more!).
- Trying to tire a dog out with more walks and more exercise doesn't work. You just get a fitter dog.
- Calmness is king. A calm dog can make better decisions.
- Start playing games at home, then gradually grow new locations as their skills increase.
- Don't be tempted to rush back to 'traditional walks'. Going slower than you think you need to will get you there faster!
- Daycare isn't right for all dogs.
- Movement helps - get them moving, keep them moving. It will help how they feel.
- You can 'change the picture' by positively introducing a new piece of equipment like a head collar.
- Don't be afraid to ask for help and support along the way. You don't have to feel alone.
- Even when you doubt yourself, or your dog, stick to the plan. Eventually, you will see changes.
- Training can take time but be consistent. And please, please believe in yourself and keep going.

18

FURTHER READING AND USEFUL LINKS

Thank you so much for reading this book. I really, truly appreciate it.

Even if you have a dog that doesn't have what might be considered 'behaviour struggles', having dogs in our lives isn't always easy. This is greatly magnified when you have a dog that does get nervous, reactive, or over-excited.

I want this book to give you hope and lots of ideas you want to try along with the confidence to know that you are not alone. You can do this!

Please take advantage of the help and support that is available to you. This can be in person or online. You do not need to feel alone at any time.

And continue to learn and inspire yourself to take a little action towards the vision you had of yourself and your pups.

A few useful links:

Pup Talk and Absolute Dogs links:

Pup Talk with Niki French Facebook group –

www.facebook.com/groups/puptalk/

Pup Talk Training Tracker –

www.pup-talk.mykajabi.com/pup-talk-training-tracker

Pup Talk The Pack membership –

www.pup-talk.mykajabi.com/pup-talk-the-pack-waitlist

Pup Talk The Podcast -

www.puptalk.libsyn.com

Sexier Than A Squirrel Podcast, from Absolute Dogs – search on iTunes, Spotify or your usual podcast platform.

Join the Worldwide Sexier Than A Squirrel challenge – 30 days, 30 games

https://go.puptalk.co.uk/sexier-than-a-squirrel-25-day-challenge/

Other links and books:

How to be a Concept Trainer - book by Tom Mitchell, BSc BVSc MRCVS

Thinking about becoming a dog trainer? Real-life results Dog Training Transformation – book by Tom Mitchell and Lauren Langman

The 100 Silliest Things People Say About Dogs - book by Alexandra Semyonova

ACE Connections Facebook group -

https://www.facebook.com/groups/332134427492077

ACE Free Work -

www.tilleyfarm.org.uk

Broken Biscuits Disabled Animal Advocacy

www.brokenbiscuits.org

Canine Arthritis Management www.caninearthritis.co.uk

Canine enrichment - Pup Talk The Podcast #33 with Kirsty Everard, Kirsty's Paws

Children and safe interaction with dogs:

I Can Be A Dog Detective! by Stephanie Zikmann -

www.facebook.com/icanbeadogdetective

Zara Dog Dog Club –

www.zaradogdog.com

Clicker Training -

https://www.clickertraining.com/15tips

Deaf Dogs and Concept Training with Natalie Rogers, K9 Concepts –

www.k9concepts.com.au/

Deaf Dogs Rock –

www.deafdogsrock.com

Health - help your dog to thrive, not just survive with A-OK9 supplements and accessories –

www.a-ok9.com/?ref=rYbcILADiwnc

Holistic Dog Grooming Academy, with Stephanie Zikmann -

https://courses.holisticgroomingacademy.com/

K9 Nation app, an online dog community –

www.k9nation.dog/

Natural long-lasting chews - Friends and Canines

www.friendsandcanines.co.uk?ref=puptalk

Scentwork - Pup Talk The Podcast #23 with Louise Wilson, Conservation K9 Consultancy

Self-care – make time for yourself. Breathwork, Pilates, stretching –

www.my-synapse.com

Separation anxiety and related behaviours – I love Julie Naismith's book Be Right Back for concentrated support with separation-related behaviours.

Sounds Scary - a free sound based treatment programme from Dogs Trust who partnered with vets Sarah Heath and Jon Bowen.

www.dogstrust.org.uk/help-advice/dog-behaviour-health/sound-therapy-for-pets

The Yellow Dog Project – check out their online store for yellow 'I need space' leads, coats etc. www.yellowdoguk.co.uk/

Toys by Tug-E-Nuff -

https://bit.ly/tugenuff1

Vidivet – www.vidivet.com for remote vet support 24/7. Peace of mind to know if your pet's health worry is urgent and needs a trip to see your local vet.

All links were correct at publication. If any links don't work for you, do please let me know at info@puptalk.co.uk

ABOUT THE AUTHOR

Niki French is a dog-mad, people-loving dog trainer and Amazon Number 1 Best Selling author with *It Starts With Me*.

Born in Keighley, West Yorkshire, Niki's favourite school holidays were on a friend's farm in Yorkshire. There were always puppies to cuddle, working sheepdogs to play with and feral cats to try and tame.

Working with animals never seemed like a reality for Niki, so she got stuck into the sales and marketing profession instead.

Fast forward 30 years to when her successful career as an international Sales and Marketing Director, was interrupted by a bicycle accident in 2014. This became the catalyst for a complete life change. It led her back to her childhood dream of working with animals and in 2019 she set up Pup Talk and Twickenham Dog Services. Her 'CEO' is Bodie, a lively young Collie Lurcher Cross, from Battersea Cats and Dog Home.

Niki is now a full-time Pro Dog Trainer. She excels at helping dog-lovers learn how to leave stress and frustration behind with simple, fun, and transformational dog training to help build a stronger bond with their pup.

Working with guardians of many breeds of puppies, nervous rescues and adult dogs with ingrained behaviour problems, Niki achieves real-life results with easy training games the whole family can play.

Niki is on a mission to give people belief, knowledge and support, and to provide the ongoing tools needed for guardians to become their dog's best trainer. She believes no dog is beyond help and is passionate that training should be an enjoyable part of daily life.

Because having a dog shouldn't be hard work.

facebook.com/puptalk

twitter.com/puptalk101

instagram.com/puptalk101

STAY IN TOUCH

If you're interested in working with me or joining the Pup Talk community, I'd love to hear from you.

Visit www.puptalk.co.uk

Email me at info@puptalk.co.uk

Follow me on Instagram and Twitter: @puptalk101

Join my Free Pup Talk Facebook group: www.facebook.com/groups/puptalk/

#trainyourdogforlife
#trainyourdogwithfun
#trainyourdogforfun

Made in the USA
Middletown, DE
11 September 2023

38013385R00116